PARAGON
ISSUES IN
PHILOSOPHY

Paragon Issues in Philosophy Series

THE PARAGON ISSUES IN PHILOSOPHY SERIES

At colleges and universities, interest in the traditional areas of philosophy remains strong. Many new currents flow within them, too, but some of these—the rise of cognitive science, for example, or feminist philosophy—went largely unnoticed in undergraduate philosophy courses until the end of the 1980s. The Paragon Issues in Philosophy Series responds to both perennial and newly influential concerns by bringing together a team of able philosophers to address the fundamental issues in philosophy today and to outline the state of contemporary discussion about them.

More than twenty volumes are scheduled; they are organized into three major categories. The first covers the standard topics—metaphysics, theory of knowledge, ethics, and political philosophy—stressing innovative developments in those disciplines. The second focuses on more specialized but still vital concerns in the philosophies of science, religion, history, sport, and other areas. The third category explores new work that relates philosophy and fields such as feminist criticism, medicine, economics, technology, and literature.

The level of writing is aimed at undergraduate students who have little previous experience studying philosophy. The books provide brief but accurate introductions that appraise the state of the art in their fields and show how the history of thought about their topics developed. Each volume is complete in itself but also complements others in the series.

iv • THE PARAGON ISSUES IN PHILOSOPHY SERIES

Traumatic change characterizes these last years of the twentieth century: all of it involves philosophical issues. The editorial staff at Paragon House has worked with us to develop this series. We hope it will encourage the understanding needed in our times, which are as complicated and problematic as they are promising.

John K. Roth   Frederick Sontag
Claremont McKenna College   Pomona College

METAPHYSICS
A CONTEMPORARY
INTRODUCTION

JOHN F. POST
VANDERBILT UNIVERSITY
NASHVILLE, TENNESSEE

METAPHYSICS
ᴀ CONTEMPORARY
INTRODUCTION

PARAGON
ISSUES IN
PHILOSOPHY

PARAGON HOUSE • ST. PAUL, MINNESOTA

FIRST EDITION, 1991

Published in the United States by
Paragon House
2700 University Avenue West
St. Paul, Minnesota 55114

SERIES DESIGN BY KATHY KIKKERT

LIBRARY OF CONGRESS CATALOGING-IN-PUBLICATION DATA

POST, JOHN F., 1936-
    METAPHYSICS : A CONTEMPORARY INTRODUCTION / BY JOHN F. POST. —
1ST ED.
        P.   CM. — (PARAGON ISSUES IN PHILOSOPHY)
    INCLUDES BIBLIOGRAPHICAL REFERENCES AND INDEX.
    ISBN 1-55778-204-0 : $16.95
    1. METAPHYSICS.   I. TITLE.   II. SERIES.
BD111.P66   1991
110—DC20   90-36424
                                                                    CIP

THE PAPER USED IN THIS PUBLICATION MEETS THE MINIMUM
REQUIREMENTS OF AMERICAN NATIONAL STANDARD FOR INFORMATION
SCIENCES—PERMANENCE OF PAPER FOR PRINTED LIBRARY MATERIALS,
ANSI Z39.48-1984.

MANUFACTURED IN THE UNITED STATES OF AMERICA

10   9   8   7   6   5   4   3   2

CONTENTS

ACKNOWLEDGMENTS

I am indebted above all to Jeffrey Poland for remarkably thorough and perceptive comments on an earlier draft. To have done justice to them all, were that possible, would have required at least another book. For further comments and suggestions, I am indebted also to Robert Audi, Jay Clayton, Paul S. Davies, Geoffrey Hellman, Ruth Millikan, Fred Sontag, and the anonymous referees for Paragon House. At those places where I have not entirely followed their advice, it is clearly at my own peril.

John F. Post

INTRODUCTION

We make sense of our lives, and of much else, largely by means of stories. Family stories help us understand where we came from, who we are, and where we might be going. So do the stories we tell about the founding of our nation and about its subsequent struggles, triumphs, and tragedies. Nor does the narrative urge stop there. So determined are we to make sense of things that we tell stories about the first human being, indeed about the origin and the nature of the whole universe. We then try to fit our personal stories into these larger ones, hoping to endow our lives with transcendent meaning.

Notoriously, stories that sustain us can also let us down. We may find that they do not correspond to reality. In my own family, my father's father got his start as a semiliterate cowboy in West Texas in the 1880s. In those days, stealing horses was esteemed about as highly as dealing drugs is today, and the punishment was appreciably more swift. Years later, Granddad Post, now settled and prosperous, decided to trace his assuredly respectable family tree, *his* father among other things having fought honorably for the South at Shiloh. But he gave up genealogy when at some point he "came across a bunch of horse thieves."

Like so many stories, this one resonates on more than one level. Not only does it poke fun at certain pretensions (though Granddad had relatively few, often telling stories like this on himself). It also says to the impressionable young listener that a measure of skepticism is in order when people strut their stories and that a sense of irony and a capacity for self-satire are likewise in order when we compose our own. The story we would like to tell could be wrong, and we should not be all that surprised if it is. Appearances are one thing, reality often another.

Many of the stories we inherit are metaphysical, in the sense that they are about the origins, the nature, the meaning, and the unity of the world. In West Texas, the inherited metaphysical story in the 1880s was drawn largely from Scripture. The world was created by God only a few thousand years ago, its plant and animal species much as they are now, its human beings dual in nature, having a material, corruptible body and an immaterial, immortal soul. The meaning of life was to be found in these terms or not at all. Hence people resisted anything that might undermine the fundamental story, including the accumulating evidence from the sciences for a much older earth, an earth on which all species, humans included, appear and evolve by purely natural means. The very distinction between the human and the animal and between the mind and the body—a distinction on which morality itself seemed to rest—was threatened and had to be protected at all costs. The offense to respectability was worse even than descent from a bunch of horse thieves, since it amounted to descent from apelike creatures no one could imagine, let alone stomach, at a family reunion.

With the advantage of hindsight, we can more readily see this episode as but one instance, though an especially trying one that is still with us, of how each generation must come to terms with tensions that arise between its inherited metaphysical stories and matters unknown or unguessed by its predecessors. Often a story must be revised or even rejected and a new tale spun to take its place—one that does justice to the novel facts and yet makes sense of the world and our place in it. Any metaphysical story worth taking seriously should therefore be contemporary: It should take full account of the wisdom of the past, certainly, but also of what has changed since then, whether in the world or in our knowledge of it.

In our day, the changes can come all too fast. Stories we told with some confidence just a few years ago may be rendered obsolete by what has happened since. In part, this is because of continuing scientific discoveries, some of them revolutionary, which have a bearing on certain metaphysical questions. Recent developments in astronomy and physics, as we shall see, can have dramatic impact on our ideas about the origins of the universe—about whether it has always existed or came into being a finite number of years ago and whether it could have had a spontaneous, *un*caused beginning or instead must have had a creator. In experimental psychology, discoveries about how we perceive things, as we shall also see, can affect our ideas about what a thing is and about why there are any things at all. Recent research into what happens in the brain when we dream may lead us to wonder whether consciousness is a matter simply of what physical states the brain is in. And we shall see how developments in biology might change our minds about the nature of language and linguistic meaning and also about the origins and justification of morality.

In these and other ways, then, we will be keeping an eye on new departures in the sciences and on why the would-be metaphysical storyteller should bear them in mind. But scientific change is not the only reason for updating introductions to metaphysics, nor is it by any means always the most important. Developments in literature, the arts, and politics can affect our ideas about the nature of what there is in the world and indeed about whether there is just one fundamental nature or essence of things in the first place. Widespread rejection of hierarchical, authoritarian political institutions and of the language of domination and priority has stimulated many thinkers to reject metaphysics itself, on the ground that metaphysic—*any* metaphysics—is inevitably committed to there being a uniquely privileged nature of things, hence to the priority of those institutions and ways of being and speaking that honor it.

Among these antimetaphysical thinkers, one finds the "deconstructionists," as they are called. According to the "deconstructionists," the metaphysician's affirmation of priority for some special way of being and talking is really an affirmation of power. This complicity with power and political will is said to reveal a readiness to do violence. The very roots of metaphysics, which metaphysicians deny or repress, include a philosophy of violence that facilitates oppression and totalitarianism. It's as though in tracing the metaphysician's family tree, what one finds is not so much a bunch of horse thieves as a bunch of imperialistic, male chauvinist brutes.

This amounts to an attack on the very idea of metaphysics—the latest in a long line of attacks. Like most, this attack proves to be based in large part on a theory of what language is and how it works. Thus we shall need to consider the merits of this and other theories of language, in light of which metaphysics is supposed to be impossible, pointless, or pernicious. We shall also need to consider whether metaphysics—any metaphysics—is inevitably committed to there being just one nature or essence of things and to some unconditionally privileged language in which to talk about it. If, contrary to the deconstructionists and others, there are varieties of metaphysics *not* committed to any such thing, as I shall suggest, then this most recent attack on the very possibility of metaphysics is wide of the mark. It's as though the posse—or rather the vigilantes—had caught and hanged the wrong party.

In addition to new developments in the arts, the sciences, and politics, there are new developments in metaphysics. One of these has to do with the relation between the being or beings a metaphysician might take as having some deep explanatory significance and all the rest of being or the beings. Metaphysics is often said to be inherently *reductive*: how everything else is must be reducible to how things are at a deeper level. The metaphysician is to give us a unified picture of the world and our place in it by showing how the many perceptible or manifest ways we and the world can be are determined ultimately by affairs at the deeper level. And the only way the one can be determined by the other, it is said, is by being reducible to it. The many manifest properties of things, ourselves included, must be reducible to properties at the deeper level in the sense that the manifest properties are really equivalent to collections or compounds of the deeper properties.

But recently some metaphysicians have suggested that metaphysical unification can be *non*reductive. There is a unity in the variety, all right, but it is not a reductive unity. The various ways we and the world can be are *nonreductively* determined by affairs at a deeper level. The key relation here is a relation of nonreductive determination. Thus we'll need to consider just what this relation is supposed to be; how it is supposed to work; and whether, as some of its critics charge, it turns out to be reductive after all.

We'll also need to consider whether talk of unification and determination, even if nonreductive, commits the metaphysician to the existence of just one nature of things and to some unconditionally privileged language in which to talk about it. Further, we'll need to examine how a relation of nonreductive determination might figure in a metaphysician's account of consciousness, meaning, value, and more. And we'll need to consider what role divinity might play in metaphysical accounts of unity-in-variety. The metaphysical storyteller can hardly afford to ignore what many think is the greatest story of all.

Along the way, we'll encounter some of the great stories metaphysicians have told, from the first metaphysicians to the latest, whether their stories are now but tall tales or sources of continuing insight and inspiration. Perhaps by the end of the book you will feel ready—and restless—to begin composing your own account of what, if anything, are the origins, the nature, the meaning, and the unity of all there is and what our place in it might be. First, however, we must consider whether such an account is even possible, or whether instead metaphysicians are pursuing a delusion. Granddad once said of someone that "he was so drunk he could see peach blossoms on a mesquite tree in January." Are metaphysicians seeing peach blossoms?

IS METAPHYSICS POSSIBLE?

WHAT IS METAPHYSICS?

Who has not wondered why we exist and where we fit into the whole of what there is? Indeed, why does anything at all exist; why not rather, nothing? Is there some real or ultimate nature of things, some hidden essence, in light of which we should lead our lives? Is there some permanent reality behind the changing appearances of things? Some cosmic design that tells us who we are and what to do? Or did the universe just "happen," having no meaning save what we supply from within ourselves?

These are a few of the questions metaphysicians traditionally try to answer. We'll look at some of their attempts in the chapters ahead. The world's great religions also offer answers to questions like these, by appealing to their founding prophets, to revelation, scripture, mystical insight. The sciences, by contrast, are supposed to make no value judgments—certainly none of the sort needed to answer metaphysical questions. Nevertheless, the sciences do tell us a lot that must be taken into account in any attempt to find answers. Astrophysics tells us a lot about the origins of the universe, evolutionary biology about how we came into being on this planet, and psychology about the roots of our thoughts, perceptions, and emotions.

What, then, distinguishes metaphysics from religion and from science? Religion and metaphysics differ in several ways, but one is especially important. It is true that members of a given religion often reflect deeply and carefully on the relations between their faith and such knowledge as we may have from the sciences, from history, philosophy, and much else. But religious reflection of this sort—however rigorous, however daring—characteristically will not allow itself to reject the basic or core beliefs of the faith within which it takes place. Such reflection is to be thought of as "faith seeking understanding," an activity from within which it is inconceivable that the understanding achieved could ever impeach the faith that seeks it.

Metaphysicians, on the other hand, require themselves to be fully self-critical, at least so far as possible, in the sense of accepting nothing as beyond question. In practice, of course, many a metaphysician has assumed various matters without argument, thinking them so basic or foundational as to require none. But in principle, at least, nothing is to be accepted simply on faith or on authority or out of inertia or failure to imagine alternatives. Instead, we are to follow the evidence and arguments wherever they lead, no matter whose ox is gored. One is reminded of Nietzsche (1844–1900): "A very popular error: having the courage of one's convictions; rather it is a matter of having the courage for an attack on one's convictions."[1] Metaphysicians need therefore to regard their enterprise with the sense of irony that comes of realizing how vulnerable one's own presuppositions can be.[2]

But is this contrast between religion and metaphysics really so clear? Doesn't there remain room, as many would argue, for *theologians*—thinkers who are *both* metaphysicians *and* of the faith? After all, the best evidence could point to the correctness of the faith in question, a possibility that should not be excluded, and a number of theologians have made profound contributions to metaphysics. True enough. But the important question is, *what is the thinker's response likely to be if the evidence happens to turn against the faith*? If your immediate response is to reject or reinterpret the evidence and defend the faith, then for the moment you are on the religious side of the divide. On the other hand, if your response is either to suspend judgment or to wonder whether the faith was wrong after all and to start thinking about alternatives, then you are on the metaphysical side; you have what is called the "metaphysical itch." Giving up a faith can be painful, even terrifying, not least because of the time and struggle needed to rethink one's life. Taking metaphysics seriously therefore demands considerable courage. One metaphysician— Santayana (1863–1952)—has even gone so far as to say, "Ah, wisdom is sharper than death and only the brave can love her."[3]

Science shares with metaphysics the imperative to go wherever the evidence leads. Nonetheless, it too stops short of adopting the full aims of metaphysics, in at least two ways. One way is to refrain from value judgments—or rather from certain sorts of value judgments, since important values guide the conduct of science, as for example in deciding which problems to work on, which ones to drop, and what methods to use. One sort of value judgment we are to renounce is whether a given fact—say, that 21 percent of American adults believe it is the sun that goes around the earth—is good or bad and what we should do about it. *No PRAGMATISTS, NEED APPLY*

Another and related sort of value judgment the sciences are to avoid involves "normative interpretation" of the facts. It is a fact that a brilliant sunset is a certain scattering of solar photons by particles in the atmosphere, or at least is caused by the scattering. But is this fact normatively more significant or more valuable than the fact that the sunset appears beautiful to us or that it may mean fair weather for tomorrow's outing? Which fact takes priority, and what kind of priority is this? Physics as physics is mute here, as is meteorology, whereas metaphysics is expected to have something to say. Likewise, evolutionary biology has nothing to say about how we should lead our lives, or what meaning they can have, in light of what seems to be evolutionary biology's own lesson that humankind evolved by accident, via the mechanisms of random mutation and natural selection.

Another way in which science stops short of metaphysics is by not inquiring into whether scientific truths represent the real or ultimate nature of the world, assuming there is such a thing, or whether they are just one among many equally privileged kinds of truth. How "fundamental" are the truths of physics, and in what sense? Do they enjoy some sort of unconditional priority over truths from other domains? In particular, is it a more basic truth that the sunset is a scattering of photons than that it means certain things to us? And what of the fact that all things in the world have various objective physical properties—mass-energy, say, or gravitational relation to neighbors, or reaction to some energy field? Does this mean that all things, persons included, are physical in nature—that they are nothing but material things? Many scientists have definite views on these issues, but not in their professional roles as scientists. Discussions of such matters are not to be found in their scientific research papers or textbooks.

Nor do scientists in their professional roles discuss the relations between science and religion, whereas metaphysicians traditionally do. Indeed, metaphysicians traditionally are supposed to say something about the relations among *all* the disciplines and further among *all* the varieties of experience. This ambition to be completely comprehensive—some would say this pretension—opens the metaphysician to ridicule in many quarters. Who, after all, can claim to know so much? Perhaps in Aristotle's day (384–322 BCE), when the disciplines were fewer and simpler, a metaphysician could plausibly claim such sweeping knowledge, but that day is long gone. Nonetheless, in later chapters we'll see how, without pretending omniscience, today's metaphysician might explain the relations among the disciplines and among the varieties of experience.

What then is metaphysics? Evidently it is the art of wondering about certain fundamental questions—questions that arise when we try to make sense of our lives—including questions about what if anything are the origins, the nature, the meaning, and the unity of all there is. Further, metaphysics is an art in which we are to follow the evidence and arguments honestly, self-critically, and with a certain sense of irony, wherever they may lead, as we attempt to form a coherent view of all there is and of our place in it. Even though the scientific facts are to be taken fully into account, we are to venture the value judgments needed for giving normative interpretations of these facts. And we are to consider whether certain kinds of truth are "basic" or "prior," scientific truth included, and to explain the relations among the disciplines and the varieties of experience.

This rough idea of what metaphysics is is not meant to cover everything that has been *called* "metaphysics," nor is it meant to preclude characterizations that emphasize other strands of the long tradition of philosophical reflection on these matters. But it does capture an important core of strands, a core that runs from Thales (early sixth century BCE) to the present and through much non-Western metaphysics as well.

Metaphysics versus Essentialism

Even so, some philosophers will object to this portrayal of metaphysics. According to them, metaphysics by its very nature is committed to much more than the portrayal implies. In particular, they believe metaphysics is committed to there being a real or intrinsic or essential nature of things, hence to there being a privileged kind of truth about the world (spiritual truth or moral or physical or whatever). Yet according to the portrayal, there could be a metaphysics committed to no such view. It says only that metaphysics is the art of wondering about what *if anything* are the nature, the meaning, and the unity of all there is. Hence the metaphysician is free to conclude that there is no such thing as *the* nature of things, *the* meaning of it all, *the* way the world is, *one* kind of privileged truth about the world. There may be many.

The issue here is largely whether metaphysics is committed to *essentialism*, according to which each thing has some of its properties not accidentally or contingently but *necessarily*, by virtue solely of being the thing it is. A property is said to be essential to a thing x when necessarily x has the property; x has the property in any possible world whatever in which x exists. These essential properties of x make up x's essence. They are often said to constitute the thing's real or intrinsic or ultimate nature.

Those who believe metaphysics is committed to essentialism tend to rely on the following account. Aristotle originated or at least defined metaphysics as the theory of being *qua* being (that is, of being as being). Metaphysicians have followed Aristotle in this regard ever since. Further, Aristotle's theory of being *qua* being was a theory of what each and every thing is essentially, *qua* itself. The metaphysician is to start by considering an individual—Jones, say—not under this or that aspect (not as student or as friend or as athlete or . . .) but simply as Jones. Next, one is to find what properties Jones has as

[left margin, handwritten:] No JUDGMENTS ARE GIVEN?

[right margin, handwritten:] WITHOUT WEIGHING REASONS.

Jones—what properties are essential to Jones's being Jones, the properties without which Jones could not exist. It follows that the inquiry Aristotle defined presupposes essentialism, and so therefore does all metaphysics properly so-called.[4]

If this historical account is right, anyone who rejects essentialism will be compelled to reject metaphysics. Many of the leading philosophers of the twentieth century do emphatically reject essentialism. Under the influence of this historical account, many of them go on to reject the whole enterprise of metaphysics; its ancestry conceals a horse thief. *But is it so clear that essentialism is presupposed by the inquiry Aristotle defined?* In particular, why doesn't *anti*-essentialism *also* count as a theory of being *qua* being?[5]

According to anti-essentialism, to be is to have no property essentially; given any being *qua* being, there is no necessary connection between it and any property it may have. There is no necessary connection between Jones *qua* Jones and any property Jones may have. There are plenty of properties Jones does have, *qua* student or *qua* friend or whatever. We may even say that Jones is "essentially human," but only so long as we recognize that this just means Jones is essentially human *qua* student or *qua* friend and that the necessity involved in Jones's being essentially human *qua* student, for instance, derives from a necessary connection *between properties*: necessarily, anything that has the property of being a student has the property of being human. This is very different from a necessary connection between an *individual* and a property. Talk of essence and accident is admissible, but only if such talk is relativized to a context in which the individual is being represented or described under some particular aspect (as student, as friend, as . . .).

Whether or not anti-essentialism is right, the fact that it can be construed as a theory of being *qua* being shows that essentialism is not presupposed by the inquiry Aristotle defined. Aristotle may be entitled to his essentialist theory of being *qua* being, but he falls short of methodological neutrality insofar as he defines metaphysics as the general theory of what each and every thing is *essentially*, *qua* itself. The kind of systematic philosophy we call metaphysics evidently is not committed to "the notion that man's essence is to be a knower of essences,"[6] though of course some varieties of systematic philosophy are so committed.

One can even argue that *Protagorean relativism* is a theory of being *qua* being and thus counts as a metaphysics.[7] Protagoras (fifth century BCE) believed that nothing exists in itself but only in relation to something else. In particular, all things exist only in relation to human perception: "Man is the measure of all things." For Protagoras, a thing has its properties not in itself, not absolutely, but only relatively; to be is to be relative. This kind of view surely counts as a theory of being as being. Thus "if metaphysics . . . is to be identified with [the theory of being *qua* being], no purer metaphysical doctrine can possibly be found than the Protagorean thesis that to be (anything at all) is to be relative (to something or other)."[8]

Note also that if relativism is right, essentialism is automatically wrong. For if a thing exists and has all its properties only relative to something else, it can have none of its properties solely by virtue of being the thing it is. If relativism is wrong, so that at least some of a thing's properties belong to it absolutely, then the debate between essentialists and anti-essentialists is a debate about whether, among the properties a thing has absolutely, it also has some essentially. All this is true not only of Protagorean perceptual relativism but of *conceptual* relativism [stimulated largely by Kant (1724–1804)]. Conceptual relativists hold that a thing does not exist in itself, or independently, but only relative to some conceptual scheme, as we see further in Chapter 4, when we discuss what a thing or a being is, and whether there is a ground of beings.

Much traditional metaphysics is essentialist to some degree. Much of it presupposes there is some one way the world essentially or really is, so that a certain kind of description is basic or privileged or forms the one true theory. Such a presupposition is said to be "totalizing" or "monopolistic." But this presupposition, like any other, is in uneasy tension with the metaphysician's own ironic imperative to be fully self-critical and to go wherever the evidence might lead. For we might be led to reject the very idea of *the* way the world is and of some uniquely privileged vocabulary to describe *the* way. That it rarely occurred to traditional metaphysicians to suspect that the

BY OUR
SOCIOLOGICAL
MENTAL SET

AS IF THE EVIDENCE
WERE NOT THEORY LADEN

evidence might actually turn against the very idea is no reason to enshrine their contrary presupposition as some sort of defining feature of metaphysics. Why define metaphysics in such a way as to prejudge one of its fundamental questions? Instead, we should think of "pluralism," as we might call it, as a logically possible metaphysical position that happened not to be filled.

ACCIDENTLY

Or at least it happened not to be filled very often. There seem to have been some pluralist varieties of metaphysics, or at any rate pluralist tendencies, that occasionally emerge alongside the more familiar totalizing or monopolistic varieties. There are pluralist themes in some Buddhist metaphysics. Among the Hindus, a thirteenth-century thinker, Madhva, holds that the properties of entities are many and diverse, that their significance is relative to some aspect or point of view from which we describe an entity, and that each entity has its own peculiar character as a result of its different relations to other entities. Similar ideas can perhaps be found in what Leibniz (1646–1716) says about the monads (units) he thinks compose the world and perhaps also in what Whitehead (1861–1947) says about the "actual occasions of becoming" he thinks compose the world. But pluralism, in the intended sense, does seem rare in Western philosophy until recently.

Traditional metaphysicians make a number of further presuppositions which are not strictly essentialist but are often associated with essentialism. Like essentialism itself, these presuppositions are not entailed by the idea that metaphysics is the art of wondering what if anything are the origins, the nature, the meaning, and the unity of all there is. Traditional metaphysicians often suppose that their theses are *necessarily* true—true not only of this world but of any possible world, unlike *contingent* theses, which are true of some worlds and false of others. Often they suppose that the theses are not known *a posteriori* (that is, only after experience or observation). Instead they are known *a priori* (that is, prior to experience) through pure reason, rational intuition, the analysis of concepts, or inference to conditions necessary for the very possibility of understanding. Often traditional metaphysicians give pride of place to matters they think are self-evidently given or present to consciousness or to the inquiring ration-

he said it,

al subject. Or the rational subject may be conceived of as known immediately and fully to itself and as autonomous or completely independent of any natural or social fabric of fellow inquirers, hence as disengaged and disembodied, standing over against a world of objects. Sometimes Platonic notions of truth, reality, and goodness are presupposed, according to which truth, reality, and goodness are transcendent objects, perhaps beyond space and time. Somehow these transcendent objects impose themselves on receptive subjects and provide unshakable foundations for all knowledge, or at least rules for reaching rational agreement. Finally, traditional metaphysicians often think of themselves as exploring a hidden, supersensible, or supernatural reality, or even a transcendental thing-in-itself behind the appearances available to common sense or to science.

In each case, there is no reason to enshrine the presupposition, however traditional, as a defining feature of metaphysics. In each case, we can imagine a metaphysics that rejects the presupposition (in light of some evidence or argument), and we can point to examples from the history of the subject that do so. But even though in each case there is a metaphysics that rejects the presupposition, *can we conceive of a coherent metaphysics that simultaneously rejects them all?* That is, could there be a coherent metaphysics that (i) rejects essentialism and the very idea of *the* way the world is, together with the idea of a privileged vocabulary to express it; (ii) consists of principles that are contingent, *a posteriori,* fallible, and revisable; (iii) involves no commitment to self-evident or other givens and none to the subject as known immediately and fully to itself or as autonomous and disengaged; (iv) avoids not only problematic notions of truth, goodness, and reality but also all talk of foundations; (v) posits no transcendental thing-in-itself beyond the appearances available to common sense and science; *and* (vi) presents an intelligible overall view of what if anything are the origins, the nature, the meaning, and the unity of all there is and our place in it? Could there be such a metaphysics? Could we use it to make sense of our lives?

Perhaps. But before galloping off like Don Quixote to find it, one should pause to ask how important it is that such a metaphysics be possible. The answer depends on how objectionable the traditional presuppositions are. The more objectionable they are, the more important it is for there to be a metaphysics that rejects them, and the harder the metaphysical Quixote must try to find it. Many philosophers now think these presuppositions ought to be rejected not just piecemeal but altogether, as we see in more detail in the next chapter. Indeed, some think the decisive considerations against them were implicit in much traditional metaphysics, so that there is a sense in which metaphysics has self-destructed. In any case, if the traditional presuppositions must all be rejected—a very big "if," according to some—and if no coherent metaphysics is possible that rejects them all, metaphysics in general is impossible. Its long history is at an end, and any further such quest is truly quixotic.

A CHALLENGE FOR METAPHYSICS

One reply to the claim that metaphysics is at an end is to defend the traditional presuppositions, and indeed some of them are far from indefensible. But there is another reply. This is to concede, if only for the sake of argument, that the traditional presuppositions lately alluded to in points (i) through (v) are to be rejected not just piecemeal but altogether, so that if no coherent metaphysics is possible that rejects them all, metaphysics is truly at an end. But having thus conceded the worst, the metaphysician could then switch from defense to offense. For suppose some variety of metaphysics *is* possible that rejects all the traditional presuppositions. Then what would be at an end would be contemporary *anti*metaphysics. Metaphysics, having weathered the worst, could press on, now purified of the objectionable presuppositions. What seemed a catastrophe would instead be an opportunity.

The trouble with this strategy is that it is vulnerable to the challenge, Put up or shut up. Unless someone can go beyond mere promises and actually offer a purified metaphysics that does the job,[9] metaphysicians had better shut up about its possibility. The antimetaphysician, defending a negative thesis (None does the job), has only to sit back and wait while the would-be metaphysician struggles to produce some such purified, constructive theory. To produce such a theory is a time-consuming matter of considerable complexity and risk. And when the brave new theory finally appears, the anti-metaphysician can easily find problems with it. Philosophical theories of large scope *always* have problems, though in this respect they are not substantially different from scientific theories of large scope. The stories we tell in order to make sense of our world, even when they are not tall tales, are never complete, never exactly right, never final.

The challenge to put up or shut up is compounded by a further condition metaphysicians themselves impose on any such constructive effort: The theory should deal with what many see as the most urgent metaphysical issue of our time. This issue, or cluster of issues, concerns the relation between a worldview derived from science and other worldviews. According to a number of influential philosophers, the sciences cumulatively tell us, in effect, that everything can be accounted for in purely natural terms. The ability of the sciences to explain matters within their scope is already very great, and it is increasing all the time. The worldview this entails, according to many, is *naturalism*: Everything is a collection of entities of the sort the sciences are about, and all truth is determined ultimately by the truths about these basic scientific entities.

A special case of naturalism restricts the basic entities to those that mathematical physics investigates (such as the various subatomic particles, force-fields, and variably curved space-time). In this version of naturalism, called "physicalist materialism," or "physicalism," everything is some collection of the basic entities that mathematical physics studies, and all truth is determined ultimately by the truths about these entities. An ancient version of materialism, due to Democritus (in the fifth century BCE), held that all is but atoms and the void. Democritean and other varieties of materialism were revived in the seventeenth century with the rise of modern physics. The success of today's physics, and of the natural sciences generally, has encouraged a number of philosophers to develop physicalism still further.

Physicalism seems to reduce all the properties of things to the properties of the basic physical entities. It seems to restrict what properly can be said of things to what can be said in the sciences. Since value judgments—religious, moral, esthetic—cannot be reduced to scientific description, they are not strictly or objectively true or false, and the values they express are not in the world but only in us. What we think of as objective values are but our inward sentiments projected onto a world which in reality is value-neutral or inert.

Furthermore, consider the subjective point of view, such as what it is like to be the persons we are, experiencing valuing and conscience as we do, and time and mystery. It seems that what it is like cannot be expressed in the sciences or in any objective idiom. For objectification omits perspective, or the subjective point of view, precisely because viewing things objectively is to view them, so far as possible, from no point of view. Thus it seems that there can be no place in a scientific view of the world for the perspective of a particular person in that selfsame world. Consciousness, intentionality, religious and mystical inner states, our experience of time—all these and more are cast adrift. Our lives can come to seem objectively insignificant, without meaning, and it becomes correspondingly difficult to commit ourselves to worthwhile projects, even urgent ones. We seem but physical objects sailing on a physical sea.

This is the stuff of alienation, but that is not the end of it. Not only are values, meaning, and the subjective point of view seemingly threatened. So too are many familiar and often cheering ordinary properties of things, such as their color, fragrance, flavor, sound, and touch. These "secondary qualities," as they are pejoratively called, are not objective or primary qualities and evidently not reducible to them. It follows, we are told, that thinking of secondary qualities as real properties of things is a "falsification of the way things are" and contributes to the "delusion that the characteristics of the universe tie in closely with the doings of human beings."[10] Thus do objectivists in general and physicalists in particular warn against the evils of anthropocentric distortion of reality and against projecting our human categories onto a world in which really there is no color, no sound, and no cheer.

How should we respond to such a worldview? Metaphysicians have wrestled with this problem at least since the rise of modern science in the seventeenth century. Today the problem seems more urgent than ever, not only because the sciences are so much more advanced but also because of the close ties between science and technology. Technology, or at least our inclination to pursue it in certain ways, results in planetwide environmental and human degradation so appalling that we are forced to question the worldview or views involved in any pursuit of that technology. Yet few wish to reject the science on which so much of the technology is based. The physics, the chemistry, the biology—even their applications—all tell us important truths about the world, ourselves included.

Small wonder that metaphysical disputes in the modern world have been said to be "fundamentally arguments for or against Materialism," with other varieties of metaphysics mostly functioning "as alternatives to this compelling, if often unwelcome, view."[11] Thus a reasonable condition—or challenge—to impose on any constructive metaphysics is that it come to terms with physicalism, either to reject or somehow to accommodate it. Then, physicalism aside, it must give a plausible account of the relation between scientific truth and other sorts of truth. In the chapters ahead we'll keep an eye on various efforts to do so.

In particular, in Chapter 5 we come across a *non*reductive version of physicalism, one that claims to give a good account of the relation between scientific and other truth. Furthermore, it claims to do so in a way that is entirely congenial to the existence and occasional priority of objective values, the subjective point of view, secondary qualities, and more; we are not nothing but physical objects storm-tossed on a physical sea. Nonreductive physicalism also claims to be a coherent metaphysics that rejects the traditional metaphysical presuppositions: It (i) rejects essentialism and the very idea of *the* way the world is, together with the idea of a privileged vocabulary to express it; (ii) consists of principles that are contingent, *a posteriori,* fallible, and revisable; (iii) involves no commitment to self-evident or other givens and none to the subject as known immediately and fully to itself or as autonomous and disengaged; (iv) avoids not only problematic notions of truth, goodness, and reality but also all talk of foundations; and (v) presupposes no transcendental thing-in-itself beyond the appearances available to common sense and science.

Whether this metaphysics is entirely successful in these and other respects is of course another matter. For now, however, having acquired some idea of what metaphysics is and of the challenges it faces, let us consider some of the arguments advanced in our century to show why metaphysics nevertheless is impossible. These arguments mostly have to do with the relations between language and reality.

NOTES

1. Quoted in translation from Nietzsche's *Musarionausgabe*, by Kaufmann (1958), vii.
2. On irony see Rorty (1989), 73, 111–112, who, however, thinks metaphysicians cannot also be ironists. He should have met my grandfather.
3. Santayana (1957), 57; the first edition appeared in 1926.
4. In this spirit Rorty (1989), 74, follows Heidegger in thinking of the metaphysician as one who takes seriously the question of what is the intrinsic nature of each thing.
5. Benardete (1989), Chs. 1–3.
6. Contrary to Rorty (1979), 367.
7. Benardete (1989), Ch. 3.
8. Benardete (1989), 16.
9. As attempted, for example, by Post (1987).
10. Smart (1963), 71.
11. Walsh (1974), 26.

2

LANGUAGE AND REALITY

LINGUISTIC ANTIMETAPHYSICS

Some things are difficult, like climbing Mt. Everest or K2. Others are impossible, like climbing an overhanging sand dune. Metaphysics, all will agree, is at least difficult, indeed very difficult. But is it really impossible? Are metaphysicians barking up the wrong sand dune? That depends on how successful are the arguments that have been brought against metaphysics. In our century, antimetaphysical arguments tend to begin by considering language, meaning, and the relations between language and the world. Because our knowledge of the world is made possible only by language, we are told, the limits on our ability to use language meaningfully to talk about the world amount to limits on our knowledge, and indeed on the world itself insofar as we can meaningfully speak of it. "The limits of my language mean the limits of my world," according to Wittgenstein (1889–1951).[1] We have access to the world, if at all, only through the veil of language.

This viewpoint resembles a story told by many philosophers ever since the seventeenth century.[2] Because our knowledge of the world is made possible only through our immediate sense experience—our sensory impressions or ideas—our knowledge of the world is limited by what we can infer from the properties of our ideas. We have direct access to our ideas or experience but not to the world itself. Unless we can somehow pierce the veil of ideas, the metaphysician's desire to talk about how things really are is doomed to failure. A number of twentieth-century philosophers replace ideas in this scheme with language as the interface between us and the world. Let us see some of the ways they have done so.

Positivism

The most famous twentieth-century antimetaphysical argument—or the most infamous—may well be one advanced by the logical positivists. They held a theory of meaning according to which a sentence or statement is cognitively meaningful only if it falls into one of two categories. The statement must be either *analytically true* (true, that is, "by definition," as supposedly are 'Bachelors are unmarried males' and '2 + 2 = 4') or else empirically verifiable or testable. The positivists arrived at this meaning criterion partly to give an account of meaning and method in science and partly to bring precision and progress into philosophy, if not to eliminate philosophy entirely. They deemed much philosophy prone to obscurantism if not outright nonsense. Metaphysics especially offended in this regard, given what struck positivists as the bombastic pseudoprofundity of its claims, or at least the claims of transcendental metaphysics about some supersensible reality. Positivists were fond of ridiculing statements such as "The Absolute is beyond time" and "The Nothing itself nothings."

Such statements clearly are not analytic. Hence they must be *synthetic*, synthetic statements being defined as those that are not analytic. But the suspect metaphysical statements are not necessary truths either. The reason is that according to the positivists all necessary truths are analytic; there are no synthetic necessary truths. Nor are the suspect statements testable by anything we could possibly experience. It follows that they are neither analytic nor testable; they are cognitively meaningless, hence neither true nor false. In the words of Hume (1711–1776), a philosophical ancestor of the positivists, metaphysics can therefore "contain nothing but sophistry and illusion," and we should "commit it then to the flames."[3]

Metaphysics was not the only victim of the positivist meaning criterion. Value judgments were also ruled cognitively meaningless and thus neither true nor false. Consider even so plain a judgment as that torturing infants is monstrously wrong. This judgment is not true simply by virtue of the meanings of the terms involved, hence not true by definition and not analytic. Nor is it empirically testable. Therefore, it must be counted not true and not false. It merely expresses an emotion—the speaker's disapproval of such torture— together with an imperative or exhortation to others to disapprove of it as well. There are no moral *facts*, no objective values, only our emotions projected onto the value-neutral real world.

Logical positivism is now almost universally thought to have failed, and not only as an argument against objective values and the possibility of metaphysics. Further study of meaning and method in science, and of the actual history of science, has shown that the meaning criterion does not yield a good account even on its home ground. Scientific statements often are not accepted or rejected on the basis of some narrow test procedure but rather in light of more global considerations (such as coherence with other science, comparative simplicity, comprehensive explanatory power, a progressive history of problem solving, and so on). Furthermore, it now appears that truth in logic and mathematics cannot be a matter simply of "definition." One reason is that the mathematical truths have been shown to outrun what can be derived from any axioms the positivists would count as analytic. Finally, there is considerable doubt whether the positivists' theory of meaning satisfies its own standard. Theories that fail to satisfy the standards they lay down for all theories are said to be self-referentially inconsistent.

All in all, positivism asserts a number of sharp contrasts, between verifiable and unverifiable, mathematical and factual, analytic and synthetic, necessary and contingent, observation and theory, the given and the conjectural, fact and value, and science and metaphysics. These contrasts have all been rejected in much recent philosophy. They are rejected even by some who wish to make philosophy more scientific or who remain sympathetic to the spirit of positivism.

One historian of twentieth-century philosophy concludes that "logical positivism . . . is dead, or as dead as any philosophical movement ever becomes."[4] As to positivism's legacy, some of it may be unfortunate—perhaps the persistent belief among some that philosophy is not about the world but about language or that philosophers should always use the technical tools of mathematical logic or that like scientists they should make no value judgments. But in the rush to bury positivism (or to heap abuse on the grave), too few reflect on the extent to which it helped render obscurantist varieties of metaphysics suspect if not meaningless, and fewer still imitate the positivists' generally high standards of argument, their intellectual honesty, and their rejection of pretentious generalizations in favor of careful attention to crucial detail.

Contingency

Ironically, a number of arguments *against* positivism, some believe, may be far more devastating to metaphysics than the meaning criterion ever was. These are arguments against the sharp contrasts entailed by positivist doctrine. One such contrast is that between the contingent and the necessary. If metaphysics must consist of principles that are necessary and if the necessary/contingent distinction must be rejected and with it all talk of necessary truth, metaphysics is impossible. So too is it impossible if and to the extent that metaphysics is committed to some notion of the given or to a sharp observation/theory distinction or to the analytic/synthetic distinction.

How might a metaphysician be committed to the analytic/synthetic distinction? One way is by construing method in metaphysics as largely a matter of *conceptual analysis*. For example, in dealing with the relations between persons (or minds) and their bodies, the metaphysician might start by analyzing various mental concepts. Just as on analysis the concept "bachelor" is found to mean "unmarried male," a mental concept such as "knows French" might be found to mean "utters French sentences on appropriate occasions." Other analyses, like this one, would be constructed out of some relatively unproblematic elements, perhaps out of terms familiar to everyone (commonsense concepts). Or an analysis might be based on terms-of-art invented on the spot to express some other fundamental matter that only the metaphysician has had the wit to see. In either case, the analysis would be presented not as empirically true but as true by virtue of the meanings of the very terms involved, hence as analytic. Thus the analysis would yield *a priori* knowledge of some necessary truth about minds, about experience, about understanding and its structures, even about the world so far as it is experienceable or intelligible.

But what is supposed to be wrong with the analytic/synthetic distinction? After all, there surely is a big difference between 'Bachelors are unmarried males' and, say, 'Phosphorus melts at 44° C'. We can easily imagine experiments that would force us to give up the latter, but what could ever make us change our minds about bachelors' being unmarried males? That's just the way we use the term 'bachelor', a convention.

True enough. But the classical analytic/synthetic distinction does not merely recognize this sort of difference between such sentences. It goes on to claim that 'Bachelors are unmarried males' is *made true* by our convention, made true not by the world but simply by our use of words, true by virtue of their meaning alone. According to the classical analytic/synthetic distinction, the difference between the two kinds of sentence is a matter of one's being made true by our meanings, the other by the world. It is this doctrine of *truth by convention* that is the target of arguments against the analytic/synthetic distinction, not the obvious fact that there is a considerable difference between the two kinds of sentence.

The most powerful attack on analyticity is that of Quine.[5] Quine argued that every attempt to provide an adequate explanation of truth-by-meaning had failed. Thus suppose I try to explain the truth of 'Bachelors are unmarried males' by pointing out that the key terms mean the same thing. Obviously I then owe you an explanation of "means-the-same," or synonymy, *and* of how it can *generate truth*. Suppose I adopt an explanation of synonymy, as many philosophers have, according to which two terms are synonymous just in case they are necessarily true of the same things. The trouble, Quine argues, is that 'necessarily true' is as much in need of explanation as is 'analytic'.

Worse, what we normally *call* necessarily true are simply those matters in whose truth we have the greatest confidence and whose role in our worldview is central; so too for what we call conventions. Notoriously, such matters can turn out to be false after all. Examples include Euclidean geometry, set theory, and the laws of elementary logic. The first, declared necessarily true by Kant, proved false of our world in light of Einstein's theory of gravitation. The second, some have speculated, may likewise need to be revised in future physics by replacing one of the axioms of what is called Cantorian set theory with an alternative. And the third, according to some physicists and philosophers, must give way to a "quantum logic" in order to resolve certain paradoxes about the quantum world.

In each case—and in many others—what once seemed true of any possible world, hence true independently of how this one in particular is, now seems no different from any other of our "high-level" theories about this world. What makes them true or false is the world, Quine thinks, *not* our conventions or meanings or some other allegedly *a priori* affair. This is the point of his slogan, "Nothing is immune to revision."

Furthermore, many things we may take to be necessarily true actually started out as generalizations about our experience of the world. 'Nothing can look reddish green' evidently is an example. Things can look reddish blue (purple) or bluish green (turquoise), but never reddish green. A number of philosophers do take it to be a necessary truth that nothing can look reddish green. But research in color vision strongly suggests that our acceptance of this truism is based on features of our visual processing that are quite contingent. Had we evolved differently, things could have sometimes looked reddish green, just as they now sometimes look reddish blue or bluish green. Indeed, in a striking recent experiment, subjects do report seeing reddish green. What seemed indubitably a necessary truth to a number of philosophers now appears not even to be true.[6]

None of this proves conclusively that the analytic/synthetic and necessary/contingent distinctions are mistakes. Conclusive proof of anything is beyond the reach of philosophy and also of science and much if not all else. But more than a few philosophers have been persuaded by these and related considerations to reject any such contrasts.

Indeterminacy of Meaning

A further consideration, also advanced by Quine, is that the very notion of meaning involved in the doctrine of truth-by-meaning is itself doomed.[7] According to Quine, meaning in the traditional sense, and sameness-of-meaning, are not empirically testable. The reason is that there can be a difference in the meaning of a couple of utterances without any appropriate difference in either the behavior or the brain or the external circumstances of the speaker or listener. Thus the meaning is not determined by such empirically testable matters as behavior, brain states, or external conditions. This "indeterminacy of meaning," when taken together with Quine's argument against truth-by-convention, would spell the end of all talk of truth-by-meaning, analyticity, necessity, and *a priori* knowledge, together with everything they imply. It would also spell the end of metaphysics if and to the extent that metaphysics is committed to any of these.

Some philosophers believe that Quine's thesis of the indeterminacy of meaning would spell the end of metaphysics in another way: It would undercut any alleged correspondence between words and the world that would entitle metaphysicians (or anyone else) to regard their utterances as determinately true of the world. Let us see how this might happen.

In a famous example, Quine invites us to consider the utterance of 'Gavagai!' by the speaker of an alien language at the very moment a rabbit bounds across the trail in front of us. We are naturally inclined to translate the utterance as 'Rabbit!' or perhaps 'There goes a rabbit!'. But the alien might be referring instead to only a part of the rabbit (an "undetached rabbit part") or to a condition or stage of the rabbit (a "rabbit stage") or even to a part of the spatially and temporally scattered object composed of all rabbits everywhere, everywhen (a part of the "rabbit fusion"). All these, and many more, are present equally. Pointing at the rabbit is simultaneously to point at them all. If we point and ask the alien, "Gavagai?" the response in each case will be yes, or what we translate as yes. There will be no difference in the alien's behavior that could determine what the referent is (rabbit, undetached rabbit part, rabbit stage, or whatever). Nor will there be any difference in the alien's brain states that could be correlated with what is being referred to: Even if there were a difference on different occasions of seeing a rabbit, the difference could as well be correlated with, say, an undetached rabbit part or a rabbit stage, as with the rabbit.

Since there is nothing else that could determine the meaning, Quine contends, meaning is indeterminate and reference inscrutable. And since all truth is supposedly determined by matters that are empirically accessible—indeed for Quine all truth is determined more narrowly still, by truth at the level of physics—it follows that there is no truth of the matter as to meaning and reference, hence none as to what the alien is talking about.

Nor are you and I in any better position than the alien. Precisely the same considerations apply to us. Hence there is no fact of the matter as to what we are talking about. If so, our words are cut off from the world. We can hardly regard them as corresponding determinately to anything in the world. Worse, once we deny determinate reference and aboutness, and with them any objective link between our language and independent reality, reality itself can begin to look problematic. If it is only relative to some interpretation of my words that it is true that there goes a rabbit, then whether there goes a rabbit seems itself to be relative to some way of interpreting or understanding. The idea of a mind-independent world begins to flicker and fade.

One widespread response to all this is to insist, "I just *know* what I mean by 'rabbit'! It's *absurd* to think otherwise, and there must be something wrong with any argument that suggests I don't!" This response seems to presuppose that I have *a priori* knowledge of meaning, knowledge that is guaranteed from within consciousness. I cannot be mistaken about what my words mean, because the meaning is self-evidently given or present to consciousness; what my words are about is a matter of what I *intend* them to be about, and I cannot be wrong about what my intentions are. The trouble with this *meaning-rationalism*, as it has been called, is partly that it presupposes a notion rejected by Quine and many others, that of *a priori* knowledge.[8] Likewise, Quine rejects any notion of a self-evident given; again, *nothing* is immune to revision.

There is another problem with insisting that I just *know* my meaning. It seems to block any account of meaning that can be smoothly integrated with what we know of human beings from the sciences. If we are naturally evolved creatures, as biology assures us, it would appear that language and meaning too have naturalistic explanations.

Now suppose we insisted that meaning is determined solely by private, self-validating acts of intending that are beyond the reach of public test. This would imply that there can be a difference in meaning even when there is no difference accessible to empirical science. It would follow that there can be no naturalistic account of meaning. Indeed, according to some philosophers—Brentano (1838–1917), for example—that is the very point of meaning-rationalism: Human beings, via language and meaning, transcend any account that would reduce intentionality to natural or causal relations of things. As Quine himself remarks, Brentano's thesis of the irreducibility of intentionality is of a piece with the thesis of the indeterminacy of meaning.[9] It's just that they draw opposite conclusions from the irreducibility: Quine, that there is no fact of the matter as to meaning; Brentano, that there can be no naturalistic science of human beings.

Perhaps neither conclusion quite follows. Perhaps there are naturalistic theories of meaning according to which meaning is irreducible to behavior, intentions, brain states, the speaker's present circumstances, or the like, and yet there is a fact of the matter as regards meaning. It turns out there *are* such theories, and we consider a couple in the next chapter. They represent important alternatives to the bleak choice between Quine and Brentano, between no fact of the matter as to what we are talking about and no notion of meaning that can be integrated with what we know of human beings from science. If some such theory proves correct, our words are not cut off from the world in the way imagined, and metaphysics is safe at least from this sort of threat.

Meanwhile, notice that even if we conclude that there is a fact of the matter as to meaning, this does not by itself restore analyticity, necessity, or the *a priori*. For the theory of meaning in light of which we conclude that there is a fact of the matter could turn out to be inhospitable to truth-by-meaning, necessity, *a priori* knowledge, and the like.

Structuralism
There are further sources of skepticism about reference and about other relations between words and the world (word-world relations).

One is "structuralism," according to which (among other things) meaning is entirely a matter of word-*word* relations internal to a language. In particular, the meaning of a word or phrase is identical with the set of its "syntagmatic" and "paradigmatic" relations, as they are called. Two words are syntagmatically related when they are arranged in sequence to make a well-formed string (a "syntagm" or sentence), as can 'cats' and 'purr'. Two words are paradigmatically related when they are associated (in memory) on the basis of some similarity or connection between the concepts they signify. For example, 'meow' is associated with 'purr', hence paradigmaticaly related to it. In English, the two words belong to an associative family evoked by 'cat'. The meaning of a word is exhausted by its syntagmatic and paradigmatic relations.

According to Saussure (1857–1913), who is widely regarded as the founder of structuralism, it follows that "Language is a system of interdependent terms in which the value of each term results from the simultaneous presence of the others."[10] Change a word's position in this system or structure of relationships with other words, and you change its meaning. The distinctive semantic contribution of each word is determined by how it differs from other words as regards the relationships they enter into in the language. "Signs function . . . not through their intrinsic value but through their relative position . . . . In language there are only differences."[11]

Some are attracted to structuralism by what they believe it implies about the world. They believe it implies that like language, the world is to be construed as "made up of relationships rather than things."[12] An item in the world, so far as we can talk about it at all, is defined not by what it is intrinsically or independently of other items nor by its "essence" (if any) but by its relations to all the other items—that is, by its relationships in a structure. The significance or sense of an item in the world is determined by the meaning of our word for it, hence by the linguistic relationships that constitute the meaning. In this view, a language creates its own reality: "Language . . . allows no single, unitary appeal to a 'reality' beyond itself. In the end, it constitutes its own reality."[13] Each society, via its language, covertly projects some such system or structure of relationships onto the

AND WHICH MAKE (with...) [handwritten marginalia]

world. There is no language-independent reality that constrains such projection (a view we encounter further in Chapter 4, when we discuss what a thing is). "Reality is carved up in various ways according to the . . . patterns of sameness and difference which various languages provide."[14] Metaphysics, to the extent it presupposes otherwise, is fundamentally misguided.

These conclusions form a version of conceptual relativism, according to which a thing does not exist in itself but only relative to a conceptual scheme. Such relativism may go beyond what Saussure himself was prepared to assert. Rather than inquire into the relation between language and reality, he seems to defer the question or to treat it as not part of the autonomous discipline or theory of language he has in mind. Within that discipline, questions about the external conditions and causes of the use of linguistic signs are to be put aside. Thus Saussure can say that his "definition of language presupposes the exclusion of everything that is outside its . . . system."[15]

Nevertheless, this official silence or agnosticism about word-*world* relations is nearly as odd in a theory of meaning as is their outright rejection. Both common sense and several theories of meaning hold that words do on occasion determinately refer to language-independent items in the world and that a word's referential function is an important dimension of its meaning. Thus the most striking feature of structuralist accounts of meaning is their omission of reference. Their notion of a linguistic sign is not one that relates a word and a thing, but rather a sound and a concept. The sign is made up of a "signifier" (a sound) and a "signified." What is signified is not some language-independent item (a rabbit, say) but a concept or idea (someone's rabbit-concept). The very identity of a concept or idea is determined by relations internal to the language: "Without language, thought is a vague uncharted nebula. There are no pre-existing ideas, and nothing is distinct before the appearance of language."[16] Whether the whole sign—the signifier-plus-signified-concept—determinately refers to some language-independent item in the world is left open by some structuralists and denied by others.

Either way, a language is treated as an entirely autonomous system, to be explained without reference to anything beyond itself. In this regard it is like chess, as Saussure is fond of saying: "Just as the game of chess is entirely in the combination of the different chess pieces, language is characterized as a system based entirely on the opposition of its concrete units."[17] The notion of "check" is entirely defined within the rules of chess; it refers to nothing beyond. We could change the rules so that the king may be taken (as in "blitz chess"); nothing external to the game constrains us. So too for language. One expositor goes so far as to say, "The word 'dog' exists, and functions within the structure of the English Language, without reference to any four-legged barking creature's real existence."[18] If so, our words are cut off from the world; there can be no hope of a notion of their being true of independently existing things. At most they are true relative to some society's way of projecting a system of relationships onto the world.

What lies behind this rejection of reference? Structuralists, even those who do not reject but are merely agnostic about reference, emphasize the "arbitrariness" of signifiers and signs. There is first of all arbitrariness in the association between signifier and signified. We could have used the sound of 'dog' to signify our concept of cats, the sound of 'cats' to signify our concept of clowns, and so on. Second, there is arbitrariness in the association (if any) between the whole sign and the real thing. "There exists no necessary 'fitness' in the link between . . . 'tree' . . . and the actual physical tree growing in the earth. The word 'tree', in short, has no 'natural' or 'tree-like' qualities."[19] Hence there is no intrinsic connection between the sign and what it means. It follows, we are told, that "the sign . . . must be defined as a relational entity, in its relation to other signs."[20] For some structuralists, at least, the arbitrariness means there can be no reference to any four-legged barking creature's real existence.

But how does it follow from the arbitrariness that the sign is related only to other signs? How does it follow that there can be no reference? One way it would follow is on the assumption that a word can refer only by somehow *resembling* or *picturing* its referent. The idea is that the word 'tree' can refer to trees only if it has treelike qualities, and 'dog' to dogs, one presumes, only if it has four legs and barks, or at least pictures or mirrors these. But this amounts to a naive resemblance theory or picture theory of reference, one which we have no reason to accept and plenty of reason to reject. There are alternative theories of reference according to which 'dog' refers to dogs without barking, and indeed without resembling or picturing or mirroring dogs in any way. We encounter two such theories in the next chapter, but we needn't accept them in order to recognize that we can use a word to refer to a thing even if we could have used it to refer to something else, and even if the word neither resembles nor pictures nor mirrors the thing. Indeed, some structuralists themselves would reject any such naive account of reference. Rather than argue that there can be no determinate word-world relation of reference, they remain officially silent on the issue.

Deconstruction

What happens to the issue in "poststructuralism," or "deconstruction," as it is called, particularly in that of Jacques Derrida? Derridean deconstructionists take over much of structuralism while questioning the rest. In particular, they question what they see as structuralism's lingering commitment to "independent meanings," in its talk of preexisting concepts as what signifiers signify. According to structuralists—certainly according to Saussure—the structure or system of concepts has a kind of transcendent ideality that exists apart from the signifiers that happen to signify the concepts. According to Derrida, Saussure "accedes to the traditional demand for . . . a 'transcendental signified'."[21] But there can be no such signified, no independent meaning or system of concepts. Rather, the signified concepts, so far from having a "commanding force,"[22] are themselves created, temporarily stabilized, and changed by the ways we happen to use words. "Language in its 'creative' uses outruns what might be accounted for in terms of purely 'structured' or pre-existent meaning."[23] Derrida excels in detailing how a seemingly necessary way of conceptualizing things corresponds to no fixed position in some independently given system of concepts. Instead, it is a quite contingent result of our habitually talking in a certain way. We could as well talk in another way, and often we should. In effect, Derrida agrees with Saussure in assuming linguistic meaning is "differential" in the sense of being determined by the relations that hold between the words in the language. But he thinks Saussure did not quite see the full implications of this move, which Derrida happily exploits to the hilt by treating the concepts themselves as differential.

Again reference drops out. Again there is silence on or outright rejection of determinate reference to some language-independent world. But now meaning is *completely* indeterminate, perhaps even more so than for Quine. There is nothing beyond our words—nothing beyond the text, no "foundation"—that could determine their meaning: not some "dictating referent that stands independent of the referring agencies of discourse,"[24] not the author's or speaker's intentions, not behavior, not brain states, and above all not some intrinsic fit or transparency between the signifier and the signified. This is the point of Derrida's famous—or notorious—slogan: "There is nothing beyond the text."[25] There is no foundation in light of which to determine the meaning of a word. The very effort to resuscitate determinate meaning is condemned as nostalgia for the lost foundation.

But what if determinate meaning is not a matter of foundations? What if determinate meaning need not be transparent or present or given to the speaking subject or to consciousness? It is true that the tradition against which Derrida is reacting presupposes some such "metaphysics of presence," according to which the meaning of an utterance is something present to the consciousness of the speaker, so that the speaker cannot be mistaken about the meaning. But it hardly follows from the rejection of such foundationalism that there can be no determinate meanings and no determinate reference to language-independent items in the world. What determines such matters might be something other than presence or any foundational affair, as we see in the next chapter.

Occasionally, deconstructionists seem to reason that because any sentence can function in many different contexts, in which it will have different meanings, it can therefore have no determinate meaning.[26] But this presupposes that a sentence would have a determinate meaning only if it expressed that same meaning in all contexts, or perhaps only if there were some one favored context in which it had that meaning. This is like saying that the word 'red' would have a determinate meaning only if it expressed that very meaning in all contexts. Yet obviously in some contexts it denotes the color, in others a member of the Communist Party, in still others a wine, and so on. Plainly, it is far more plausible to say that in each context of use 'red' has a determinate meaning, even though there is no one meaning it has in all contexts. If you and I are discussing wines and you say, "Try the '73 red," then in this context 'red' certainly seems to denote a wine, and determinately so.

There is a similarity between what motivates the foregoing argument from multiple contexts against determinate meanings and what motivates the structuralist's uneasiness about reference. The idea in both cases is that there would have to be some nonarbitrary, necessary connection between a word and what it determinately means. In the present case, the alleged necessary connection is held to be destroyed by there being no one favored context in which the word has a meaning. A word has no "essence," hence none that ties the word to the extralinguistic item or items it might denote, nor do the extralinguistic items themselves have an essence that could bind certain words onto them. The resulting arbitrariness is supposed to imply that there can be no determinate meanings. But why should we suppose that the only way words can correlate with or map onto meanings or onto the world is via some such necessary or essential tie? Again, there are plausible theories of meaning that require no such tie, as we see in the next chapter.

Actually there may be a reason why structuralists and deconstructionists alike suppose there must be some such necessary connection between a word and what it means. They may have been influenced by meaning-rationalism, as we called it earlier, a view that recurs in much Continental philosophy (but not only there). They may share the meaning-rationalist's presupposition that if there are determinate meanings, the subject must have *a priori* knowledge of them. They may believe further that such knowledge could only be gained by way of some appropriate necessary connection between the word and what it means; otherwise the word's meaning could not be suitably present to consciousness, as it must be if the subject is to have *a priori* access to the meaning. Since there is no such necessary connection, hence no such presence, there can be no *a priori* knowledge of what a word means, hence no determinate meaning at all.[27]

This line of thought is no stronger than the meaning-rationalism that underlies it. Perhaps there is an alternative account, as we see in the next chapter, according to which meaning is determinate but not known *a priori*, and the determinacy is not at all a matter of presence. Instead, we can sometimes be mistaken about what we mean, hence mistaken about what we are thinking.

REALISM

We have been considering a number of arguments against the possibility of metaphysics. Each is a special case of a more general strategy common to much twentieth-century philosophy. The strategy is to begin with a philosophy of language or theory of meaning, then use it to evaluate and typically to deflate the claims of metaphysics. Undoubtedly this can be a healthy corrective to occasional pretentious extremes. More often, however, the deflating can get out of hand, as when we seem driven by considerations about language to question the existence of a largely mind-independent world. We may seem driven by worries about determinate reference to question whether there really goes a rabbit or by the arbitrariness of language to conclude that reality is relative to each society's linguistic projection.

The fact is that philosophies of language—including theories of meaning, of reference, of truth, and the like—belong to one of the most controversial and least understood fields of inquiry about human beings. If not still in its infancy, it is also not yet beyond a troubled adolescence. Inferring from a theory of language to the nature of what there is in the world would seem one of the more problematic inferences of our time. Surely we ought to have more confidence that there are rabbits and rocks, people and planets, than that our favorite theory of meaning is the last word. Likewise we may surely be more confident that rabbits and rocks do not depend for their existence or all their properties on our consciousness or conceptual scheme or language. So says *realism about the world.* Yet many philosophers seem inordinately fond of reversing the matter. For many of them, *anti*realism is motivated and allegedly justified by various theories of meaning. This is one reason why, in order to understand contemporary metaphysics, one must also understand some philosophy of language.

Not all varieties of metaphysics are realist. They do not all hold that there is a largely mind-independent world of objects like rocks, trees, other people, and more. The contrary view—*idealism*—rejects realism about the world. Most idealists do not go so far as to reject the very existence of rocks, trees, and other people—what philosophers with their usual sensitivity and discrimination often lump together as "the ordinary furniture of the world." Instead they believe the furniture is mind-dependent.

One way in which things can be mind-dependent is expressed in a famous saying of Berkeley (1685–1753): *"Esse est percipi,"* meaning "to be is to be perceived." Nothing can exist or have the properties it has except as it is present or presentable to some mind or minds. Berkeley did allow that things are not always perceived by a *human* mind; what saves them from nonexistence is being perceived by God. Most contemporary idealists, however, who tend to be conceptual relativists, dispense with God so far as this sort of salvation is concerned. Nor do they often require things actually to be present to a human mind; some require only that they be presentable, others that they be dependent on the mind in some other way.

Because realism is ridiculed in much contemporary philosophy, and because it nevertheless seems so sensible and innocuous, one wonders whether what is being attacked as realism is a scarecrow. Setting up a scarecrow is a fallacy of reasoning, according to the textbooks (though they still call it the "straw man" fallacy). Nevertheless it is all too prevalent among philosophers, who ought to know better. We set up a scarecrow when we make a position into something other than what it really is or implies and then use the substitute to scare everyone off, typically by arguing that it is defective in some way. Such scarecrow tactics are not always deliberate. They can result from careless or unsympathetic reading of the opposition, from stereotyping, *or* from the failure of the opposition *itself* to distinguish clearly between the required core of its position and what is optional.

Realists themselves have not always been completely clear about what is required and what is optional. But then their attackers also have not been notably energetic or charitable in separating the realist wheat from the chaff. Let us begin to do so here, by noting some propositions which realism about the world does *not* imply, contrary to many of its critics.

Essentialist?

First and foremost, perhaps, realism does *not* imply essentialism. To say that a stone exists and has many of its properties independently of our consciousness, language, or interpreting activity is not to say that it has these properties necessarily or essentially. For recall our discussion of essentialism in Chapter 1. There we noted in connection with Protagoras that if relativism is right, essentialism is automatically wrong. But we also noted that essentialism could be wrong in another way: If things do have at least some of their properties absolutely—that is, not relative to or dependent on something else, human beings in particular—still they need have none of them necessarily or essentially. This is fundamentally why realism does not imply essentialism.

Nor does realism imply that there is just one way the world is. It does not imply that there is some account of the world that excludes all others, the one true and complete description or theory of the world's furniture.[28] The stone can be many ways; it can have many kinds of properties, or at least there can be many different kinds of truth about it. Not only does the stone have a certain shape and mass, it has a certain texture, reflectivity, and color. It also bears various relations to its surroundings, such as the relation of being on the shore or under water or once part of someone's house. If we allow that being on the shore is a property of the stone—meaning a *relational* property—the stone could have this relational property and many others in virtue of its relations to a wider environment. If we deny that so-called relational properties really are properties of the stone, as some philosophers do, we can at least say it is true of the stone that it bears these relations to other things. It might even be true of the stone that it was the one used by David to kill Goliath or that it was deemed holy by some now-vanished people or that I intend to place it over the mantel. These truths and others like them would express some significance or sense or meaning the stone has.

It seems, then, that there are many ways the stone is, at least as many as there are kinds of truth about it. No such description is "more true" than any other; none takes some unconditional priority over the others; none represents either the essence or some one "absolute version" of the stone, the exclusively true account couched in terms of a "final vocabulary."[29] Or if you believe the contrary, it would have to be on the basis of something other than the belief simply that the stone exists and has many of its properties independently of our awarenesses or conceptualizations of it.

One reply to all this is that whether they like it or not, realist metaphysicians *are* committed to the priority of independent or objective existence. Why else would they begin by urging our attention to it? They seem to have been captivated by a distinction between inner and outer—between an inner, subjective, human world and an outer, objective, impersonal, anonymous world. They then opt for the primacy of the outer, objective world. That they do accord primacy to the objective world is shown by how they always begin their story with objectively or independently existing things and by how they frequently try to reduce or unify everything in terms of the objective. The result is a kind of hierarchy of what there is, grounded ultimately in the outer world. Or so it would appear.

At this point some philosophers simply reverse the priority, awarding the prize to the inner world, as does Husserl (1859–1938) and other phenomenologists. Often they do so in the name of protecting the inner "life-world" against what they see as an objectivizing science that is hostile to authentic human being. In *their* hierarchy, everything—science included—is grounded ultimately in something to do with the inner life-world. Or if not strictly the inner world, then at least in some aspect of human being. The ground might have to do with conceptualization or understanding or as in Heidegger (1889–1976) with how we interpret everything according to its meaning for human being.

But must we choose? Perhaps neither inner nor outer has unconditional priority and likewise neither some aspect of human being nor some aspect of nonhuman existence. Indeed, a few philosophers seem to reject this whole game of awarding priority to one pole or the other of the inner/outer polarity and like polarities. One way to do so is by appealing to Wittgenstein, who taught that there are many equally privileged ways of talking. Each of these "language games" has its own vocabulary and rules. None represents some alleged ultimate structure or exclusive account either of the world or of human-being-in-the-world or anything of the sort. Taking this clue to heart, a philosopher could then argue that neither a language game about the outer, objective world nor one about the inner, subjective world is prior or basic or foundational.

Derrida, perhaps unwittingly echoing Wittgenstein in this regard, "deconstructs" the inner/outer distinction, meaning among other things that the alternatives are to be treated as "equi-primordial."[30] This seems to mean in turn that neither takes unconditional priority over the other; each in some sense is "founded" in the other, hence founded in "what it excludes." Instead of merely *reversing* the priority together with the hierarchy built on it, we are to reject all such hierarchies. By insisting on priority or primacy, we subordinate one to the other and thereby seek domination over the other. The game of awarding primacy is thus essentially political. The metaphysician's affirmation of priority is really an affirmation of power. And this complicity with power and political will reveals a willingness to do violence. Therefore, deep down in all metaphysics there lurks a philosophy of violence that would make common cause with oppression and totalitarianism. Or so we are told.[31]

Some varieties of metaphysics may well be guilty of such sins. But are they all? For example, is a realist metaphysics in fact committed to the unconditional priority of the so-called objective world? Apparently not. To say simply that there are mind-independent entities and properties does not by itself imply that they enjoy any such priority. The realist could even argue that whatever priority the objective world may have is highly *conditional*, meaning that *if* in a given context we are interested in what exists independently of our understanding or interpretation or consciousness, *then* such matters enjoy a certain priority, but it will always be only priority-in-a-respect. In the context of doing physics, let us say, for the purpose of finding a particular kind of very general explanation of certain phenomena, we are often interested in finding independent or objective relations among and laws about events—relations and laws that obtain regardless of one's perspective or frame of reference (as we see concretely in this chapter's concluding section). On such occasions, the independent or objective relations and laws take on a corresponding sort of priority, perhaps a kind of explanatory priority.

On other occasions, the independent or objective matters are not what take priority. For example, suppose we are interested in the nature of the *evidence* for the existence of these objective matters. Then the subject's observations, among other things, take on a kind of priority—call it *evidential* priority. Or we might become interested in how we manage to refer to or talk about the events studied by physicists. Then such "intentional" matters as aboutness and reference take on what might be called *semantic* or *referential* priority. Or we might want to understand what it is like to be this or that particular subject, in which case various matters take on some sort of "phenomenological" priority. And so on.

The realist could even argue that there is no such thing as unconditional priority. Instead, priority is *always* only priority-in-a-respect, in a certain context for some purpose or relative to some interest. "No order has absolute priority over any other. . . . Priorities of all kinds there surely are . . . but all are conditional. . . . Priority [is] always priority in some respect."[32] As for the objection that after all the realist begins with objectively existing things, the realist could reply that we have to begin *somewhere*, as when we slice a pizza, and that the pizza can be sliced quite equitably wherever one starts. We could equally well start with evidential matters, or phenomenological, so long as we do not lose sight of the independently existing world of other people and things. The realist insists only that no matter how we slice it, independently existing things must be given their due along with everything else. So long as the inner world is likewise given its due, by way of emphasizing its appropriate sort of priority (or priorities), where we begin is unimportant.

Totalizing?

Realism sometimes is accused of being a totalizing or monopolistic view, in the sense of wanting to reduce the multiplicities of experience to a single, comprehensive, underlying unity or whole.[33] Again it should be clear that nothing of the sort is entailed. To say simply that there are mind-independent things is not to say or imply that everything can be unified in terms of them, reductively or otherwise. Whether they can is a further question. True, some realists have indeed tried to unify the phenomena reductively, in terms of various mind-independent entities. Traditional materialists, for example, have tried to do so in terms solely of basic physical entities, Pythagoreans have tried to do so in terms of number, event-ontologists in terms of events, process philosophers in terms of becoming, and so on. But unification need not proceed by way of reducing the phenomena to the chosen class of entities, as we'll see in detail in Chapter 5.

Moreover, whatever realists themselves may sometimes have thought, the existence of a kind of unity in the world does not by itself exclude the coexistence of *other* kinds of unity, which on occasion may be just as important if not more so and may enjoy a corresponding sort of primacy. Any contrary claim to exclusive truth or primacy would of course be totalizing or monopolistic, but nothing of the sort is entailed by realism properly so-called. If one is leery about realism on the ground that it is necessarily reductive or totalizing, one has been put off by a scarecrow. The same is true if one thinks realism lends comfort to *scientism*,[34] according to which everything must be reducible to a purely scientific account of us and the world.

Slave to Common Sense?

Nor does realism about the world imply that ordinary or common-sense entities or beings like stones, trees, and people are the *only* things there are. There could also be many extraordinary "things" like quarks, fields, "quantumstuff," variably curved space-time, and black holes. At least there could be such things if what is called *scientific realism* is right. The scientific realist holds that the "theoretical entities" talked of in physics and the other sciences exist. Further, some realists believe that mathematical entities exist, perhaps beyond space-time. Some believe that other such abstract entities exist—propositions, properties, possible worlds. And some believe in God. Others believe in all these things and much more.

Noumenal?

Talk of noumena goes back to Kant. Kant accorded a much more active role to the mind than did Berkeley. The world as we perceive it—the phenomenal world—is produced by a kind of interaction between mind and the raw material provided by the reality on which mind operates. Certain categories of our understanding and forms of intuition are imposed or projected on this reality, which in itself, as it truly is, is unknowable. For example, the reason everything we encounter in experience exists in space and time is that the mind is constructed in a certain way. Items or aspects of the raw material on which the mind works are experienced only if and to the extent that they can be presented by the mind in spatial and temporal guise. The mind imposes spatiality and temporality on the raw material. The raw material itself—what Kant called the things-in-themselves, or the *noumena*—cannot be said to be either spatial or temporal. Crudely speaking, it's as though we were at the bottom of a well covered by a grating—the mind—with the noumena on the other side. Only those noumena (or rather their aspects) that fit the grating get through. They are the phenomena that bombard us below. What we ordinarily *call* the real world—the phenomenal world—is constituted by the interaction of mind with an unknowable beyond.

Does realism entail that there must be some such transcendental reality beyond or behind the furniture of the world—beyond the stuff that gets through the grating? Must there be some noumenal realm behind the phenomena we call rocks, trees, minds, quarks, or space-time? Not at all.[35] Of course realism does entail that there is something beyond our consciousness and our language-driven conceptualizations of things. Thus realism entails that there is something that transcends mind, in the sense that there are objects that exist and have many of their properties independently of our experience, consciousness, categories of understanding, or use of language. But what is said to be there independently are good old rocks, trees, friends, and so on, not some unconceptualized—let alone unconceptualizable—noumenon or thing-in-itself or some "noumenal dough" waiting to be shaped by the mind into "objects." True, realists do sometimes talk of how things are in themselves, apart from our conceptual activity, and some of them have indeed posited a noumenal realm. More often, however, their talk of how things are in themselves is just an abbreviated way of talking about how some things exist and have many of their properties independently of our consciousness, of our language, and so on.

Final?

Realism does not mean that everything we *think* is real or mind-independent must *be* so. No present inventory of what there really is should be thought of as final. A sense of irony becomes the realist, who is likely to mine history for examples of our recurring fallibility. For instance, everyone once thought that any two events occur simultaneously or not, irrespective of the frame of reference of the observer. It turns out that according to Einstein's special theory of relativity (STR), they are *not* simultaneous *period*, but only relative to a frame. If you blink your eyes, the two eyeblinks are simultaneous for you but not for someone on a spacecraft hurtling inbound from Mars at an angle to your line of sight.

The old realism about simultaneity evidently was mistaken. Physics, via STR, has replaced it with a realism about a relation between events that *does* hold independently of an observer's frame. This relation is the "space-time interval," defined in analogy with the notion of distance between two points in space. Such a relation is said to be an *invariant*, meaning roughly that it obtains and has a certain magnitude independently of the choice of coordinate system, reference frame, or perspective. Einstein never liked the term 'theory of *relativity*', evidently because his is basically a theory of space-time invariants (*"Invariantentheorie,"* as he at first called it). Indeed, physics in general aims in this realist way at finding the invariants in the phenomena. It even uses such invariance as the very criterion of what really or independently exists.

Take another example. Until recently everyone thought—and

some still think—that every particle always has a determinate position irrespective of our measurements of its momentum. This is a kind of realism about a certain property of the particle, namely its position. But according to quantum theory (on its usual interpretation), the particle cannot *have* both determinate position and determinate momentum at the same time. The more precise a measurement of the momentum, the more "smeared out" the position, and vice versa. Realism about such "incompatible" properties evidently has proved mistaken.

Does this mean that quantum theory shows that realism in general is wrong? Not at all, no more than STR shows it wrong by discovering the relativity of simultaneity. Even according to quantum theory, the particle does have some properties that are the same under all measurement conditions, or measurement-independent. These are the "static properties," such as rest mass, charge, and spin magnitude. Moreover, the basic equations of quantum theory are themselves taken to describe relations that hold independently of measurement or the observer, including the very relation of incompatibility between position and momentum. The theory is therefore in large part about certain invariants, thus furthering a fundamental realist aim of all physics. And if quantum theory ultimately compels us to reject all talk of *particles* as measurement-independent entities, as some believe, the realist may cheerfully go along, agreeing that what does have such independent or real existence is instead "quantumstuff," say, or infinitely large, indivisible, dynamic fields, or whatever. What physicists and philosophers of physics often *call* "realism" and argue is shown wrong by quantum theory is not realism proper. What they call realism is a view according to which position, momentum, and the like must be real properties of particles. Even if realism about such properties is wrong, realism need not be.

These, then, are some of the propositions that realism about the world does *not* imply, occasional appearances to the contrary notwithstanding. A number of them, perhaps all, have been rejected at one time or another by various philosophers on the basis of some philosophy of language, including the language of physics. But even if this sort of inference from a philosophy of language to the falsity of the propositions in question were sound, still it would not follow that realism is wrong. For realism does not imply any of these problematic propositions, though certainly there are scarecrows in the neighborhood that do.

On the other hand, nothing in this chapter explains how, if at all, we succeed in saying things about the mind-independent matters the realist metaphysician insists there are. What positive account, if any, could the realist or anyone else give of how we are to pierce the veil of language and say something true about reality?

NOTES

1. Wittgenstein (1961), sec. 5.6, first published in 1922.
2. Hacking (1975).
3. Hume (1955), 173; first edition, 1748.
4. Passmore (1967), 56.
5. Quine (1976), first published in 1936; and Quine (1961), first published in 1951.
6. Crane and Piantanida (1983); Hardin (1988), 121–127.
7. Quine (1960), (1969), (1970).
8. Millikan (1984), 10, 91–93, 326–333, argues that Quine nevertheless remains a meaning-rationalist, because he believes that knowledge of synonymy, could we but have it, would have to be *a priori* knowledge.
9. Quine (1960), 221.
10. Saussure (1966), 114; first French edition, 1916.
11. Saussure (1966), 118, 120.
12. Hawkes (1977), 17.
13. Hawkes (1977), 26.
14. Norris (1982), 5, who attributes this view to Saussure.
15. Saussure (1966), 20.
16. Saussure (1966), 111–112.
17. Saussure (1966), 107.
18. Hawkes (1977), 17.
19. Hawkes (1977), 25.
20. Culler (1976), 36.
21. Derrida (1981), 19–20; first French edition, 1972. Ellis (1989) is probably the best accessible critique of deconstruction.

22. Lentricchia (1980), 161.
23. Norris (1982), 52.
24. Lentricchia (1980), 167.
25. Derrida (1976), 158; first French edition, 1967.
26. As Nehemas (1987), 35, suggests.
27. This seems to be the line taken by Culler (1982), 92–96.
28. Contrary, apparently, to Putnam (1983), 210–211.
29. Rorty (1989), 75–77, thinks that realists and indeed all metaphysicians are committed to some such final vocabulary.
30. On the relation between Wittgenstein and Derrida, see Rorty (1984), 5.
31. Derrida (1978), 97, 141.
32. Buchler (1978), 577–578.
33. An accusation found for example in Putnam (1983), 226.
34. As does Putnam (1983), 198–199, 210–211.
35. Contrary, apparently, to Putnam (1983), 210, 226.

force a group to accept yr pt.

3

PIERCING THE VEIL OF LANGUAGE

TRUTH AND METAPHYSICS

Like everyone else, metaphysicians want their beliefs to be true. But true in what sense? Necessarily true? Monopolistically or exclusively true? True in the sense of corresponding to how things are in the world? In the sense rather of corresponding to *the* way they are? In the sense of being verified or warranted by the evidence to date? Of cohering with the whole body of all our beliefs? Of being what our friends will let us get away with saying? None of the above?

Each of these possibilities represents a particular theory or account of truth. This includes accounts according to which truth is not the sort of thing about which we should expect to have some deep theory; 'true' is just the compliment we pay to the sentences we happen to accept. Which account should we believe?

Note first that metaphysics is not committed to any particular account of truth. Some metaphysicians are committed to one, some to another, some to none at all. Consequently, objections to any given account of truth spell no trouble for metaphysics as such, but only for those varieties (if any) that happen to adopt that account. At the same time, metaphysicians do want to say something about extralinguistic matters, even if there is no agreed sense in which what they say of them is supposed to be true. Earlier, we saw how Quine, the structuralists, and the deconstructionists all question the very idea of a determinate tie of aboutness or reference between words and the world; they are by no means alone in doing so. Rejecting determinate reference would undermine metaphysics to the extent that metaphysical assertions—indeed, *any* assertions—are to be determinately about matters beyond language or beyond the text. Rejecting determinate reference would also undermine certain accounts of truth, *realist* accounts in particular, according to which a true sentence is made true by something in the world, not by our evidence and not by consensus, coherence, interpretation, linguistic projection, or conceptual scheme. Realists about truth believe that truth is a word-*world* affair, not word-word, and in such a way that the conditions of truth are in the world, not within the mind.

Like realism as regards the world, this realism as regards truth is distinguished by a kind of "declaration of independence": Truth is independent of such perspectival or mental matters as consensus, interpretation, possession of evidence, coherence with our other beliefs, or conceptual scheme. But even though realism as regards truth and realism as regards the world share this declaration of independence, neither entails the other. It is possible to be a realist about the world and also an antirealist about truth. Many philosophers believe that there are mind-independent items in the world but not that true sentences are made true by them. It is possible to be the reverse: a realist about truth yet an idealist about the world; a true sentence is made true by items in the world, yet the items are mind-dependent. Or one can be a realist in both senses or in neither.

In the previous chapter we noted how shaky is the inference from certain theories of meaning to antirealism about the world. By contrast, the inference from them to antirealism about truth is in much better shape. The question is not whether antirealism about truth follows from them—mostly it does—but whether they are adequate as accounts of meaning. If not, they provide no reason to reject realism as regards either truth or the world, hence none to reject those varieties of metaphysics committed to either sort of realism.

Theories of meaning that would eliminate reference usually begin by supposing or arguing that the alleged reference of a bit of language, like all meaning, must be determined by a certain kind of fact. They then explain how the reference is not determined by such fact and conclude there can be no determinate relation of reference between words and the world. For example, recall how Quine supposes that meaning, hence any alleged reference, would have to be determined ultimately by the behavioral or at least by the neurophysiological states or dispositions of the speaker. He then explains, via the "Gavagai" example, how such matters do not after all fix the reference. They could be the same yet the reference varies, between rabbits, their stages, undetached parts, and so on. The conclusion is that there can be no determinate relation of reference. Reference is inscrutable, and inscrutable for the simple reason that there is nothing there—no determinate reference—to scrutinize. Structuralists and deconstructionists afford another example of the same general strategy. They suppose that all meaning is determined by certain word-word relations internal to a language. Since reference is not so determined, the conclusion to be drawn is either agnosticism about or outright rejection of any such word-world relation.

What these strategies suggest is that reference is not determined without remainder by anything "in the head": not by brain states, not by dispositions to behave in certain ways, not by our associations of words with certain words, not by any mental imagery we may have that seems to be "of" or to "present" the alleged referent. Auxiliary arguments suggest further that reference is also not determined by our intentions. An additional argument, advanced by Putnam, seems to many to seal the verdict that, as he puts it, " 'meanings' just ain't in the head."[1] Imagine that far, far away there is a planet called Twin Earth, molecule-for-molecule just like Earth, as are the people on it. Each of us has a Twin-Earth double whose behavior, brain states, awareness, word-word associations, and conscious intentions are the same as ours. So too do the Twin Earthlings include among themselves speakers of a language phonologically and syntactically the same as English. In circumstances in which we would utter 'There goes a rabbit!' our Twins would too. But it happens that Twin rabbits, though otherwise like Earth rabbits, are made not of carbon-based organic molecules but silicon-based. Hence Twin rabbits are not rabbits. Whereas our utterance refers to a rabbit, the same utterance by our Twins refers to a Twin rabbit; the reference is just not the same.

Putnam's ingenious bit of science fiction is widely taken to show that reference does not depend solely on—is not determined without remainder by—the speaker's word-word associations, behavior, imagery, or mental states, intentional or otherwise. For these are all the same on Twin Earth as here. Yet the reference differs: Our Twins are talking about Twin rabbits, we are talking about rabbits. Meaning, in any sense that could determine aboutness and reference, "just ain't in the head." If one adds to this the assumption that *it cannot be anywhere else*, as at least implicitly do Putnam,[2] Quine, the structuralists, and deconstructionists, it follows that there can be no determinate reference relation between words and the world.

There are philosophers who would reverse this verdict. There *is* such a relation, all right, but it is not to be found in the head. Those who assume it cannot be anywhere else seem to do so under the influence of meaning-rationalism. They think that speakers would have to have *a priori* knowledge of what they mean, and the only way to have such knowledge is for the meaning to be in the head or mind, where the speaker can have *a priori* access to it. Contrary to this meaning-rationalism, the moral of Twin Earth, we are told, is not skepticism about reference but skepticism about meaning-rationalism and about theories of meaning that reduce meaning to what is in the head—to the speaker's associations of words with words, to brain states, imagery, dispositions to behave in certain ways, to intentions, or whatever. The problem, of course, is to say just what reference does consist in, if not some such intracranial affair. Solving this problem is necessary if metaphysicians wish to pierce the veil of language—not in order to look on reality bare, whatever that would mean, or to have the things-in-themselves presented to consciousness with dazzling immediacy, but simply to say something determinately or objectively true of what there is.

CAUSAL THEORIES OF REFERENCE

One possibility is that reference consists in a kind of *causal* relation between my use of a word and whatever in the world the word thus used refers to. After all, if we are naturally evolved creatures, language presumably played a causal role in our evolutionary success. It did so by enabling humans to communicate essential information about their world to each other, as when a returning hunter-gatherer scout tells about game or forage or shelter over the horizon. This "telling about," like everything else that evolved, must emerge from and somehow be explained by the web of causal relations we call "nature," or perhaps "nature-plus-creature." According to this line of thought, there has to be a causal relation that underlies our success in telling each other about our world.

Naturalistic reflections like these are a large part of what motivates causal theories of reference, though some philosophers become causal theorists for other reasons. Causal theories of reference hold that a word refers to whatever is causally related to it in an appropriate way. The simplest case is that of a proper name. Suppose we are given a pet rabbit which we decide to dub 'Thumper'. We see the rabbit and are thereby causally affected by it, as is our use of the name 'Thumper' at the dubbing. In this way a causal link is established between the rabbit and our use of the name. The reference of 'Thumper' is fixed and would be understood by anyone who witnessed the dubbing. Later, someone not a witness might be told the name in conversation and thereafter use it too. Via the conversation and the dubbing, a causal chain connects this later, remote use with the rabbit. The reference of the later use is thus borrowed from the first or dubbing use. After a few such borrowings, a speaker who uses the name 'Thumper' may know little or nothing about what it names and indeed may be under the false impression that it names a ruffed grouse or an untuned motorcycle. Nevertheless, the name does continue to refer to the rabbit, not to whatever the speaker happens to have in mind. What determines the reference is not in the speaker's head but in the appropriate causal chains, so that the speaker can be quite mistaken about the reference, contrary to meaning-rationalism.

Causal theorists extend these basic ideas, with suitable amendments, beyond names to other sorts of terms—to kind-terms such as 'rabbit', mass-terms such as 'gold', and more. They also elaborate the theory to deal with ambiguous terms, with terms whose reference changes, and with terms that have no referent. The theory is capable of far more sweep and subtlety than the present sketch could possibly convey.[3] But it is already clear that such a theory is a naturalistic account according to which meaning, in the sense of reference, is irreducible to behavior, intentions, and the rest. Yet there is a fact of the matter as to meaning. The theory thus provides an alternative to both Quine (no such fact of the matter) and Brentano (no naturalistic science of human beings). Because any word or sound can be causally linked with a given object in the world, which word we use is arbitrary, and there need be no resemblance or picturing or mirroring between word and object or any necessary or essential tie between them. Our words are not cut off from the world in the way envisaged by many antimetaphysicians. Further, the way is open to a realist account of truth, according to which the truth-value of a sentence is determined by how things are with the objects to which its terms determinately refer by way of the appropriate causal chains.

Unfortunately, there are some problems for causal theories of reference. One has to do with abstract entities like sets, numbers, and properties. If such abstracta exist, as even some naturalistically in-clined metaphysicians think, they seem not to be in space-time and thus not capable of entering the appropriate causal relations. Yet we certainly seem to refer to them in mathematics and elsewhere. In reply, the causal theorist might argue that there are no such abstract entities in the first place, thus siding with nominalists against realists as regards abstracta. Our seeming reference to them is a mere manner of speaking. There are several quite respectable programs for thus "nominalizing" mathematics and other discourse which the causal theorist could take over for this purpose.

Another difficulty concerns events so remote in space-time that no causal influence—not even light—can reach us from them. Recall Einstein's special theory of relativity, introduced in Chapter 2. It is a consequence of STR that there are such events—events outside our "backward light cone." In STR, therefore, we refer to such events even though we cannot be causally linked to them. In reply, the causal theorist might argue that reference to such events is achieved by use of a *kind*-term—a term that refers to a whole *kind* of entities. The kind-term might be 'event separated from us by a spatiotemporal interval'. There is no requirement for everything that satisfies a kind-term actually to be connected to us by a causal chain. The kind-term is normally "grounded" in the world by perceptual contact with a few *samples* of the kind, which does require actual causal connection of these samples to us. The term's extension—the set of things it is true of—is simply the set of all those things of the same kind, in this case events in space-time. Thus we can use the term to talk about things in its extension whether or not we are connected to all of them by some causal chain, hence whether or not they are outside our backward light cone.

A more serious problem for causal theories is the *qua* problem. When we dubbed Thumper 'Thumper' we were causally related, via perception, not only to the whole rabbit but also and equally to a stage of the rabbit, an undetached rabbit part, a member of the set of rabbits, a part of the rabbit fusion, and so on (as we saw in effect when discussing Quine's argument for the indeterminacy of translation in Chapter 2). Presumably it was Thumper *qua* rabbit we dubbed 'Thumper', not *qua* rabbit stage or the rest. But what, if anything, determines this? In virtue of what was the name grounded in Thumper *qua* rabbit? Appeal here to a causal link will not help, since all are equally causally linked via perception to our use of 'Thumper' in the act of dubbing. A witness would have no way of telling which it was. This problem might be called Quine's revenge against causal theories of reference, in view of its similarity to his argument for the inscrutability of reference. It could equally well be called Brentano's or Husserl's revenge, in view of their insistence (and that of other phenomenologists) that no purely *causal* account of meaning will do.

In response to the *qua* problem, some causal theorists have concluded that "there must be something about the mental state of the grounder that makes it the case that the name is grounded in the cause of the perceptual experience *qua whole object.*"4 The grounder must "think of" the cause of the experience under some specific description such as 'whole object' or 'whole animal'. The result is a descriptive-causal theory, not a pure causal theory. A term is associated, consciously or unconsciously, with a description in a grounding. 'Thumper' is associated with some description such as 'whole animal' when the causal link is established between Thumper and the name 'Thumper'. In some sense speaker and witness have reference-fixing information to the effect that Thumper is a whole animal and not a part of one or a stage or whatever. What determines the reference of 'Thumper' is this information plus the causal connection it selects. In the present case, the connection selected is with Thumper *qua* rabbit rather than *qua* rabbit stage, undetached rabbit part, or the like.

This is a big step toward putting meanings back in the head. Worse, for the causal theorist, some account would need to be given—presumably a causal account—of how it is that the grounder's mental state determines that the relevant causal connection is the one between the name and the whole object. This was the very kind of problem that causal theories were supposed to solve or bypass in the first place. For this reason, as well as for some others, not everyone is persuaded by this response. Nor are they persuaded that a causal theory, even if it is revised to deal with this specific difficulty, can provide an ultimately satisfactory account of reference. Is there an alternative? There are several, but one in particular deserves attention here.

BIOSEMANTICS

"Biosemantics" refers to an approach developed by Ruth Garrett Millikan.[5] It too is naturalistic. Also, it entails that there is a fact of the matter as regards reference and rejects any reduction of meaning to brain states, dispositions, word-word associations, imagery, or speaker's intentions. Nor does it require any resemblance or picturing or necessary tie between a word and an item in the world. Further, it rejects meaning-rationalism; knowledge of meaning is not *a priori* knowledge, and we can indeed be mistaken about what we mean. But instead of starting with dubbing and causal chains, as do causal theories, Millikan invites us to step back and consider the problem in a broader perspective.

When we look at the evolutionary history of our own and other species, we are struck by the way in which various behaviors and devices, including those we might call signing behaviors and devices, have functions or purposes important to the success of the species. When a bee returns to the hive it does a certain "dance," one that is correlated with the direction in which it found nectar. The device or mechanism that produces the dance, like the one that interprets it, has the function or purpose of causing other bees to fly in the right direction. The dance is "about" the direction, or at least it correlates with or maps onto the direction (different dance variations correspond to different directions; the duration of the dance corresponds to the distance). If the dance did not so map, the outward-bound bees could not perform properly in finding the nectar. Of course, the bees are not aware that the dance so maps. They simply react appropriately to a certain stimulus, when all goes well.

This example and many others prompt the speculation that one of the functions of the devices in humans that produce and interpret speech in the form of sentences is to produce and interpret sentences about affairs in the world. A sentence maps onto a specific world-affair in a way more complicated than, but not unrelated to, how the bee's dance maps onto a certain direction. If a returning hunter-gatherer scout's sentences did not map onto food or shelter over the horizon, the band would be that much less likely to find any. Thus "a very tempting theory of man's knowledge is that it consists in part of inner 'maps' or of inner 'representations' that model man's outside world inside him."[6]

How can we tell which sentences map onto which world-affairs? Consider an analogous question about the bees: How can we tell which dances map onto which directions? In the case of the bees, at least, one is tempted to answer that we can tell just by looking. We merely correlate a specific dance with the direction the bees actually take. But even here there is a problem with this sort of answer. For the bees may not always go in the right direction, and indeed sometimes they do not. Other factors may intrude: defective or diseased dance-interpreting devices, direction finders, or flight mechanisms; unfavorable external conditions (wind too strong, alien queen nearby); and so on. Furthermore, there may be mistakes made in the dance itself.

To discover the correct mapping or correlation, therefore, it is not enough simply to average over actual behavior. Such averaging may put us on the right track, but we must go further to find the *rule* to which the bee's actual behavior is *supposed* to conform. For the returning bee, let us say the rule is "When nectar bears 50° from the sun, dance Opus II, no. 4." For the outward-bound bee let us say, "When they dance Opus II, no. 4, fly 50° from the sun." The actual rule is much more complex.

Thus there is a *normative* element involved in the idea of the correct mapping. There is a direction a given dance is *supposed* to map onto and the bees then take. We find out what the dance is *supposed* to map onto not simply by averaging over actual behavior or even dispositions to behave and not by peering into the bees' heads. Instead, we guess at—that is, we form hypotheses about—the proper function of the dance in relation to various positions of nectar, hive, and sun. And of course we must first have guessed at the general function of any such dance behavior in the life of the hive.

This problem of discovering proper function is common in biology. Thus consider the hoverfly.[7] Males of many species of hoverfly hover for hours in one spot, occasionally darting after various targets (passing midges, small windblown objects, male hoverflies, distant birds, female hoverflies). What are they doing? That is, what is the proper function of this behavior, what biological purpose does it have, what rule or rules might be involved? It turns out that the males are "keeping their flight muscles warm and primed so that they are ready to dart instantly after any passing female they sight. This chasing behavior is on such a hair-trigger that all manner of inappropriate targets elicit pursuit."[8] Calculation shows that in order to intercept the target, the hoverfly must turn at an angle equal to the angle between the center of his retina and the image of the target, $-\frac{1}{10}$ the image's angular velocity, $\pm 180°$. According to Collett and Land, the hoverfly does indeed conform to this rule. Because it is a rule about how he should respond to a proximal stimulus (the moving spot on his retina), Millikan calls this "the proximal hoverfly rule."

Conforming to this proximal rule is a means of conforming to a less proximal, more distal, rule: "If you see a female, catch it." A still more distal rule might be "Propogate the species." Such rules represent biological purposes the hoverfly has. They are *unexpressed* purposes, indeed purposes of which the hoverfly is not and could not be aware, given his relatively simple nervous system. Nor could they be found by peering into his head. Instead, to say that he has such a purpose is to say that "[he] has within him a genetically determined mechanism of a kind that historically proliferated in part [among his ancestor hoverflies] *because* it was responsible for producing conformity to the . . . rule."[9] In order to find out the purpose or function of some behavior or device—to find the rule or rules to which it conforms and sometimes fails to conform—we must often take a long look back in time to see what role it played in such evolutionary success as the creature may have enjoyed. In doing so we discover "how purposes inform the rule-following behavior of the hoverfly, how norms, standards, or ideals apply to his behaviors, hence how the hoverfly comes to display competences or abilities to conform to rules rather than mere dispositions to coincide with them."[10]

It is instructive to consider whether at this point Quine could raise his concern about indeterminacy. According to Quine, we recall, meaning is indeterminate because it is not determined by the speaker's or hearer's actual behavior or dispositions to behave. It is also not determined, he would likely say, by the behavior or dispositions even of all *past* speakers or hearers; no bare appeal to history, therefore, can reinstate determinacy. So too, surely, for the rules to which the hoverfly is supposed to conform.

In particular, consider the proximal hoverfly rule, "Turn at an angle equal to the angle between the center of the retina and the image of the target, $-1/10$ the image's angular velocity, $\pm 180°$." There are *other* rules that fit all past hoverfly behavior and dispositions *just as well as this one.* One such rule would be

If the image's angular velocity is less than $10^{10°}$ per second, turn at the angle between the image and the retinal center, $-1/10$ the image's angular velocity, $\pm 180°$; at ease otherwise.

Since never in history has a target's image had an angular velocity of this super magnitude (we may assume), this rule—call it the *quoverfly* rule—fits all past hoverfly behavior and dispositions exactly as well as the proximal hoverfly rule does. Therefore, the correct rule, even if there were such a thing, is not determined by the behavior or dispositions to behave even of all past hoverflies.

This would be to misconstrue Millikan's thesis. The thesis is *not* that the correct rule is the one that fits or is determined by all past behavior or dispositions to behave, even when such behavior and dispositions contributed to hoverfly procreation and survival. Rather, the correct rule is the one conformity to which explains how the hoverfly's male ancestors (or enough of them) managed to catch females and proliferate. The added business in the quoverfly rule— the business, *"If the image's angular velocity is less than $10^{10°}$ per second . . . ; at ease otherwise"*—does no work in the *explanation* of how the hoverfly's ancestors proliferated. For consider a parallel case. The explanation of why my jacket keeps me warm is not that it is down-filled *and red*, and not that it is down-filled *if the temperature is less than $10^{10°}$ C*, but just that it is down-filled. The italicized material here does no work in the explanation and can simply be dropped. It is a superfluous complexity that can be eliminated "without affecting the tightness of the relation" between the explanation (being down-filled, turning at a certain angle) and what is to be explained (keeping me warm, hoverfly ancestors' success in procreating).[11] Thus it is the hoverfly rule, not the quoverfly rule, that is the correct rule, the one the hoverfly has a biological purpose to follow.

Like remarks apply to the bee's dance. We assumed that the correct rule—the rule the bee is supposed to follow—is one according to which a certain dance correlates with or maps onto a certain direction to the nectar. But there are also indefinitely many *other* mappings we need to consider, such as the one between the dance and the direction to an undetached nectar part or to a nectar stage or a part of the nectar fusion or whatever. All these mappings or correlations are present equally. What, if anything, determines that the correct rule, assuming there is one, is the one according to which the dance maps onto a direction to the *nectar*? This is the *qua* problem all over again. Quine would say that the alleged correct rule is not determined by the bees' actual behavior or dispositions to behave, not even that of all past bees unto the beginning of the species. Nor is it determined by the physical states of their nervous systems. Since there is nothing else that could do the determining, in Quine's view, there is indeterminacy here and hence no fact of the matter as to what the correct rule is. There is only the veil of bee dances.

According to Millikan's biosemantics, however, there *is* something else that is relevant, namely the biological explanation of honeybee survival via their success in nectar gathering. The correct rule is the one conformity to which explains how the bees' ancestors (or enough of them) managed to fly in the direction of nectar so that the species proliferated. The business about an undetached nectar part, nectar stage, part of the nectar fusion, and so on does no work in this explanation and should be dropped as a superfluous complexity. The *qua* problem, and Quinean indeterminacy, are thereby blocked, according to biosemantics.

So far we have been considering *innate* or *wired-in* biological purposes and competences to conform to a rule. There are also *learned* competences and *derived* rules—something *new* under the sun—to which the creature may henceforth conform or fad! to conform. Millikan's example here is the rat. Upon becoming ill within a few hours of eating a specific substance, rats will thereafter shun anything that tastes the same. In doing so they are following "the proximal rat rule": Don't eat what tastes like the stuff you had when you got sick. Conforming to this rule is a means to conforming to a more distal rule, perhaps "Don't eat poisonous substances."

Now suppose the rat becomes ill after eating some of the children's silly putty, a substance rats have encountered nowhere in their evolutionary history. In order to conform to the proximal rat rule, the rat must now conform to a further proximal rule, "Don't eat what tastes like silly putty." This is a *derived* rule, and the rat learns a new competence to follow it. "In this manner, animals that learn can acquire biological purposes that are peculiar to them as individuals, tailored to their own peculiar circumstances and peculiar histories."[12] A chimpanzee who learns sign language, as a number now have, learns to produce a certain sequence of signs to get a certain food, another sequence in the presence of a certain state of affairs, and so on. The chimpanzee acquires a competence and a purpose to conform to a number of derived rules. In this case, these are rules that involve correlations or mappings between certain sequences of signs and certain states of affairs. "What an organism does in accordance with evolutionary design can be very novel and surprising, for the more complex of nature's creatures are designed to learn."[13]

Now consider, from this biological point of view, the human use of sentences. Sentences, like bee dances, have biological purposes or functions (among others). The sentences produced by the hunter-gatherer scout on returning to the band have the purpose or function of "adapting" the listeners to certain world-affairs or conditions. This enables the listeners to pursue their purposes in line with just those conditions, thus enhancing their chances of success. The sentences perform this function by virtue of mapping onto conditions or world-affairs in conformity to certain mapping rules. The mapping rules, not unlike those for bee dances, are rules in conformity to which "a critical mass of sentences have mapped onto affairs in the world in the past, thus producing correlation patterns between certain kinds of configurations of sentence elements and certain kinds of configurations in the world."[14] The correlation patterns enable the listeners to adapt their activity to the configuration or world-affair thus mapped and thereby to improve their chances of success. An adequate explanation of their success would have to make reference to these correlation patterns, much as an explanation of the bees' success in finding nectar refers to the correlation between dance and direction. Complexities that do no work in the explanation cannot be used to argue that there is indeterminacy as to what the correct mapping rules are.

The *qua* problem, and Quinean indeterminacy, are thus blocked much as before. We can tell what the mapping rules are, and which sentences map onto or correspond to which world-affairs, by looking back in time to discover which rules and which correspondences explain what the hunter-gatherers are doing and explain this without superfluous complexities that play no explanatory role. So too do we look at a history to find the rules, proximal and distal, that explain what the bee, the hoverfly, the rat, and the chimpanzee are doing. We are likely to find that a certain bee dance maps onto a direction to nectar, not an undetached nectar part, and that a certain sentence maps onto a world-affair that involves a rabbit, not a rabbit stage, whereas another sentence maps onto one that involves the stage, not the whole rabbit.

The speaker need have no description in mind, and no conscious intention or other mental state, with which the key term in the sentence is associated. The speaker needs this no more than the bee does when a dance maps onto a direction to the nectar rather than a direction to an undetached nectar part. On this theory, the *qua* problem is solved, or rather can scarcely arise, because the biology-inspired methods and explanations we are to use lead us naturally to the rule to which a given device or bit of behavior is supposed to conform. Of course the methods and the rule are sometimes quite complex, and we can sometimes be wrong about what the rule is. But this sort of fallibility is common to all empirical investigation and implies no difficulty-in-principle for biosemantics.

What determines what a given sentence is about, then, and the reference of the terms in it, are explanatory facts about a history in which certain sentences in the past, and derivatively their terms, have come to have a certain purpose or function, as has the bee dance. This purpose or function is a matter of these past sentences' correlating with certain world-affairs and of their terms' correlating with aspects of those affairs. What the mapping rule is for a given sentence today which also contains these terms is determined by these correlations between its terms and the aspects in conjunction with semantic rules that project, from the terms and the structure of the sentence, the conditions under which it would be true. In this way, *novel* sentences—sentences never produced before—can also map onto world-affairs. The theory also makes provision for novel terms.

In the first instance, therefore, whole sentences are what map onto or correspond to a world-affair. "A less direct, more mediated, kind of correspondence is the correspondence between a referential term *in the context of a true sentence* and its referent."[15] The relation between a lone term or a term in a false sentence and its referent is even more derivative. It is the relation not of actually corresponding to something but of there being something to which it is *supposed* to correspond. Yet doubly derivative though this relation is, there is a fact of the matter as to what a given referential term refers to, via the determinacy of the mapping rules for the true sentences in which the term occurs. In this way 'Thumper' does indeed determinately refer to Thumper.

What makes a given sentence true is that there is something in the world—a world-affair, a configuration, a condition—onto which it maps in accordance with a certain mapping rule. There need be no one kind of condition onto which sentences always map—no one way the world is, no absolute version.[16] Nor need the rule be something in the speaker's head, no more than the proximal and distal rules to which the male hoverfly conforms need be in his head, or the bee-dance rules and mappings are in the bees' heads. Moreover, the mapping rule governs the manner in which sentences are supposed to correspond to affairs that are very often well beyond the mind or the interface between mind or body and world. Indeed, the affairs mapped may be so distant that no causal chain connects them to the speaker. There need be "no causal relation whatever between the representation and what it represents."

It follows that the mapping rule is not a proximal rule but a distal. So too for truth-rules, therefore, which are those "that project, from the parts and structure of sentences in a language, the conditions under which these sentences would be true" or that map sentences onto their truth-conditions.[17] When sincere speakers make assertions, their purpose is to make true assertions, hence to conform their sentences to these truth-rules. The rules need not be expressed or expressible by or known to the speaker, no more than the bee's rules need be expressible by or known to the bee. Yet we can usually tell well enough whether the speaker has the competence to conform to the rules. That is, we can tell whether the person has the requisite linguistic competence.

It follows from all this that truth-rules are realist or correspondence rules, not rules about what goes on (or ought to go on) in the mind or the body. Nor are they rules about verifiability. They govern the way in which assertions are to correspond to conditions that obtain in the world beyond. Not only can we be mistaken about whether the conditions obtain, we can also be mistaken about what the truth-conditions of a given sentence are. In this sense we can be mistaken about what we mean, since the rules that govern what a sentence means are not known *a priori*.

Such, in broad outline, is biosemantics. What its reception will be is hard to anticipate. Potential critics have not yet had the time for thorough evaluation, and in any case biosemantics differs in fundamental ways from established accounts of meaning and truth. It calls for a largely new way of thinking about these matters, a basic shift in the paradigm. Such shifts always make it hard for the established disputants to understand the new theory, let alone agree with it. But whatever its ultimate fate, the theory offers an account of how human beings have all along succeeded in saying things determinately about particular aspects of the world and how, therefore, a metaphysician could do so as well.[18] If the theory is right, language is not a veil between us and what there is, but a remarkable, naturally evolved device for talking about what there is.

Those who reject metaphysics on the basis of theories of meaning that eliminate determinate aboutness and reference must henceforth take account of Millikan's theory. Hers is a naturalistic theory of aboutness and truth, realist in character (and also nonreductive, as we see in Chapter 5). There need be no such thing as *the* way the world is, or some one true and complete description of the world. Likewise there need be no totalizing or monopolistic unification of everything in terms of some one kind of truth. Nor is there any appeal to a transcendental or noumenal reality, beneath or beyond the furniture of the world, as that which makes a true sentence true. The furniture itself will do nicely. And there is no implication—quite the reverse— that every sentence we *think* has mind-independent truth conditions must have them.

These are some of the things Millikan's realism about truth does not imply. They parallel the propositions, considered in Chapter 2, that are not implied by realism about the world. Nor are they implied by some other versions of realism about truth. Yet realism as regards truth, like realism as regards the world, has often been rejected altogether, along with any metaphysics that presupposes it, on the ground that it implies some or all of these problematic propositions. Of course there are scarecrows in the neighborhood that do imply them, but again this is no reason for wholesale rejection. Metaphysicians, like all human beings, seem able to say things that are determinately true of the world. Let us resume considering some of the things they have said, starting with why there is a world at all.

NOTES

1. Putnam (1975), 227
2. Millikan (1984), 326-333.
3. Devitt and Sterelny (1987).
4. Devitt and Sterelny (1987), 64.
5. Millikan (1984), (1989).
6. Millikan (1984), 8.
7. Another of Millikan's examples, developed at length in Millikan (1990).
8. Collett and Land (1978), quoted in Millikan (1990), 331.
9. Millikan (1990), 331-332.
10. Millikan (1990), 337 In.
11. Millikan (1990), 334 In.
12. Millikan (1990), 339 In.
13. Millikan (1989), 292.
14. Millikan (1984), 99.
15. Millikan (1984), 104.
16. Millikan (1984), 109.
17. Millikan (1990), 334.
18. Millikan (1984), Chs. 15-19.

4

WHY DOES ANYTHING AT ALL EXIST?

A TRADITIONAL ANSWER

We might have been born of different parents or in a different land, and it seems only by luck that we are who we are. Indeed, we need not have been born at all, and the queasy realization that we might not have existed can make us wonder why we do. But the question of why we exist is ambiguous. On the one hand, it could be asking for the purpose or purposes for which we exist, assuming there is some purpose, or for some mission or meaning in light of which to lead our lives. On the other, it could be asking for an *explanation* of our coming to be, hence for an explanation of why we exist. Let us reflect awhile on this second way of taking the question. The other way of taking it is just as important, if not more so, but we delay returning to it until later in this chapter and in the Epilogue.

When we ask for an explanation of our coming to be, the answer is likely to begin with something about how our parents met and how they came to have children. But just as there is nothing necessary about our own existence, there is nothing necessary about our parents' existence either. So we may wonder in turn why and how *they* came to exist, and before them *their* parents, and so on. Soon we may find ourselves wondering why there are any human beings at all, and why there is an Earth for them to inhabit. As Aristotle put it long ago, "At first people wondered about the more obvious problems that demanded explanation; gradually their inquiries spread farther afield, and they asked questions upon such larger topics as changes in the sun and moon and stars, and the origin of the world."[1]

At each step of the way in this sequence of why questions, we assume that there is indeed an explanation for what we are wondering about, even if we do not know what the explanation is. We may not know why the Earth came to exist, but we are confident there is a reason. And astrophysics does seem to confirm our expectation by explaining how the formation of a star like our sun normally involves the formation of planets and how in the case of our sun certain conditions existed that led to the formation of the Earth.

There is a general principle at work behind our belief that there will always be some explanation, even when we do not know what the explanation is. The principle is that for every contingently existing thing or event or state of affairs, there is an explanation of it in terms of something that necessitates its existence or occurrence. This principle is a version of the classical "principle of sufficient reason" (PSR). PSR is illustrated—and presupposed—by the inquiry into why the space shuttle Challenger exploded. The commission of inquiry assumed that there were causal factors that obtained just prior to the explosion and necessitated that it would occur. The question was only *what* those factors were. The commission found them in the O-rings, the cold weather, and questionable management practices. This example and many others like it seem to show that PSR is presupposed by all scientific inquiry and by common sense. In the next section we consider whether PSR *is* presupposed by science and whether it is true. For now let us assume PSR is true. After all, as common sense assures us, it seems simply incredible that something—anything—could just happen, with no cause.

Little wonder, then, that when people begin to ask not only of the Earth and the sun but also of the whole universe why *it* exists, they automatically assume there must be some explanation. The universe, all hands agree, might not have existed, so it is a contingently existing thing. According to PSR, therefore, there must be some explanation of why it exists; it could not have just happened, it could not exist uncaused. Furthermore, the explanation apparently must be in terms of something else—something beyond the universe. The reason is that the notion of explanation relevant here is one according to which the explanation of a contingently existing thing is in terms of some *other* thing. It would be odd to say that the explanation of why the Earth exists has something to do with the Earth itself, as if somehow the Earth existed by a necessity of its own nature. Apparently, "The explanation of one thing is another thing," as Bertrand Russell (1872–1970) once put it.[2] It follows that the explanation or cause of the universe's existence, if there is an explanation, would have to be something beyond the universe, something beyond space-time altogether. According to traditional theism, there is indeed something beyond, and this cause or creator is God.

Some have objected to this theistic account that the universe might well have no beginning. The universe might always have existed, so that no matter how far back in time we go there is an earlier state of the universe, one that explains the existence of the next state. But this objection is flawed. There is first of all the problem of whether the universe has in fact always existed. Here the evidence is less than compelling, to put it mildly (as we see in the last section of this chapter). Further, even if the universe has always existed, we would still have to face the question, Why does this *always-existing* universe exist, why not another one or nothing at all? Theists often emphasize this question, not least because they think they have a ready answer: It exists because of God's creative activity. God made it the case that there is such a universe, though we are not to think of the divine act of creation in terms of a temporal causal process in which an earlier event or state causes a later one.

Nor are we to think it necessary for God to have created what happens to be the actual universe rather than some other. God created this world, not another, through a freely chosen act of creation. Nevertheless, though it is not necessary for this world to have existed or for God to have chosen it, there is a sufficient explanation of its existence in terms of God's creative activity. God's free choice, together with God's power, necessitated the existence of just this universe.

Note also that the reference to God is supposed to put an end to the regress of why questions, in which each answer to why is greeted with a further why. For God is said to be a *necessary* being, not contingent, in the sense that God exists in every possible world whatever. The principle that every *contingently* existing thing has an explanation in terms of something beyond is not to apply to God. Moreover, God is said to be necessary also in a second sense, according to which God's very nature entails God's existence. It is of God's essence to exist, which is to say that God is the sort of being that exists by some necessity of its own nature. Therefore, those who grasp the concept of God as a necessary being will automatically understand why God exists. They will understand this not in terms of the causal or creative power of something allegedly beyond God but in terms of God's own nature or essence. Asking why God exists would be rather like asking why a plenum is full; the very concept of a plenum requires that it be full.

It follows that even if we believe not only that every contingently existing thing has an explanation but also that everything whatever does, the question of why God exists still has an answer in terms of God's own nature. The regress of why questions is therefore supposed to end with God.

There is a problem about God's own free choices. It seems to make sense to ask why God makes those choices and to expect that there is some explanation of this even if it is not an explanation known or knowable to us. That is, it seems that PSR applies to God's free choices. But does it? If they are contingently occurring affairs, PSR requires that there be something beyond them that necessitates their occurrence. In that case, it is hard to see how they would be genuinely free. Suppose instead that they occur not contingently but necessarily, in the sense that the very nature of the choices entails their occurrence. Then there is an explanation of their occurrence in terms of their own nature or essence, but again it is hard to see how they would be genuinely free.

Some theologians and philosophers—the "compatibilists"— argue that even if PSR applies, so that the choices have a sufficient explanation or cause, they are nevertheless free; freedom is compatible with such explanation and causation, hence with PSR. But some others, many theists included, choose to say instead that at least where God's free choices are concerned, PSR does not apply. There is and need be no explanation, known or unknown, of their occurrence, though there is an explanation of the occurrence or existence of everything else either in the causal power of something beyond or in a necessity of the thing's own nature.

We have been tracing the traditional theist's answer to the question of why anything at all exists. The sum total of contingently existing things exists ultimately because of God's free creative activity, and God exists by a necessity of God's own nature. Asking why God exists is like asking why a plenum is full: Asking just shows that you don't understand the concept, either of a plenum or of God. Furthermore, theists will claim that there is a bonus in their answer to the question of why anything at all exists. It *also* answers the question in its *other* sense or senses—that is, when it is about the meaning of life and the purpose or purposes for which we exist. The meaning and the purpose are contained in God's reasons for creating a universe and the beings in it, reasons that are the subject of divine revelation.

PRINCIPLES OF SUFFICIENT REASON

Does everything have a cause? It can certainly seem so. Even when we do not know just what the cause is, we are sure there is one. We are so sure, in fact, that even if we find no cause after years of searching, we blame our lack of knowledge, not the world. We think that if we could only learn more about the relevant causal factors and the laws that govern them, we could give a complete causal explanation of the unruly phenomenon. It has even been said that "Seek causes" is a fundamental imperative of scientific method.

PSR is so deeply entrenched in our view of the world that many philosophers have held not only that it is true but also that it is necessarily true—true not merely of this world but of any possible world. Further, its truth is known not as a result of empirical investigation but *a priori.* In much the same mood, other philosophers have asserted that PSR is "a presupposition of reason itself"[3] or that PSR is of the very essence of rationality. When Sartre (1905–1980) declares existence irrational and absurd, he does so partly on the ground that were existence rational it would have an explanation (by reference to some Necessary Being); since it has none, it is irrational and absurd.

The first cracks in the united front of belief in PSR probably began to appear in the 1920s, a time of revolutionary developments in physics. In order to construct an adequate theory of many new and puzzling atomic and subatomic phenomena, physicists like Heisenberg and Schrödinger worked out equations that proved to fit the observations with startling accuracy. Furthermore, by relying on the new equations, physicists were led to predict a number of hitherto unsuspected phenomena. The predictions were amply confirmed by subsequent experiment. The old Newtonian physics soon seemed obsolete to many physicists, at least when it came to accounting for these micro matters. The new "quantum mechanics" began to look like the only game in town, and in the decades since then the mounting evidence has only confirmed its triumph.

The shock was that the new equations entail what is called "quantum indeterminacy," which we encountered toward the end of Chapter 2. If we assume that the equations are true of the world, as the evidence powerfully implies, and if we give the equations their usual interpretation, then at some deep level the world must be nondeterministic. Events can and do occur that are not completely determined—not caused—by any antecedent physical events or states of affairs.

For example, consider a beta particle created at a particular instant during the spontaneous decay process within the nucleus of a uranium atom. Quantum theory, under its usual interpretation, assures us that the existence of *this* beta particle at *this* instant is *not* necessitated by what is going on in the nucleus. It *is* necessary that some beta particle or other would be created over a period of time but not that any would be created at the instant of the beta particle in question. It is not even highly probable that any would be created at this instant. Nor is this indeterminacy or "uncertainty" a matter of our not knowing enough about the factors involved. Even if we knew all about them, the indeterminacy would remain. The existence of this particular beta particle is not necessitated by the relevant factors, not because we do not know enough about the world but because the world is that way. The existence of this particle *has* no explanation, known or unknown, in the sense of explanation meant in PSR.

Or rather it has no explanation in physical or natural terms. We could of course postulate some supernatural cause of this particle, some divine loading of the dice, so that PSR is satisfied after all. But we would have to do so for each of the countless billions of other spontaneous quantum events, and in any case such a move seems strained, artificial, ad hoc. We could save any hypothesis we like by postulating supernatural intervention in just the right way at just the right moment. For example, we could save the hypothesis that impure thoughts are what cause acne by supposing that a supernatural being forges a link between the two that is invisible to medical science.

It seems safe to say that if today's physics is right, PSR is wrong, unless someone can show that the seemingly spontaneous quantum events all have some supernatural cause. This would not be the first time a general principle based partly on earlier science was undermined by later science. Nor would it be the first time philosophers' entrenched intuitions about an alleged necessary truth foundered on the rocks of empirical inquiry, as in Chapter 2 we saw of Euclidean geometry and of the belief that nothing can look reddish green. Moreover, the idea that PSR is a presupposition of reason, so that to be a rational person is to accept PSR, is also in deep trouble. For it is clear both that a rational person could be led by the evidence and arguments in physics to reject PSR and that nonetheless it would be rational for such a person to continue to rely on evidence and argument. Whatever precisely we mean by rationality or rational method, PSR is not presupposed by it. It follows that if something turns out to have no explanation, this does not mean that it is "irrational" or "absurd" in the sense of not conforming to some alleged norm of rationality.

But if PSR is wrong and there are uncaused events, what happens to the imperative to seek causes? Should scientists and others now stop looking for them? Not at all. To seek causes does not commit us to believing there must always be a cause for us to find, no more than seeking gold commits us to supposing there will always be gold where we hope to find it. Often there will not be. On such occasions the better part of wisdom is to admit it and look elsewhere. Science does not presuppose PSR, even though science is an enterprise dedicated in large part to seeking causes.

If not everything has an explanation and PSR is wrong, what happens to the question of why anything at all exists? Suppose the question means, What is the explanation of why anything exists? Obviously this presupposes there *is* an explanation. But without PSR to rely on, we have no guarantee that there must *be* one; the presupposition that there is could be false. And if there need be no explanation, there need be none in terms of God's creative activity. This spells trouble for a certain kind of theism, according to which belief in God is supported in part by the idea that reference to God is necessary in order ultimately to answer the question of why anything exists. For suppose this question is based on a false presupposition. Then it is out of order in the same way the question, When did you stop beating your spouse?, is out of order. Attempts to answer it are misguided, and alleged answers to it afford little or no support for belief in God.

Theists might reply that however things go at the micro level to which quantum theory applies, still the *universe* at least is the sort of thing that has an explanation, hence the sort of thing to which PSR applies. Even if there need be no explanation for the emission of a beta particle at a given instant or for other spontaneous quantum events, there must be one for the existence of the universe. The best explanation at this level is in terms of God.

There are at least two difficulties with this reply. One is that physicists have begun to apply quantum theory to the universe as a whole. Some physicists even argue that the evidence to date implies the universe had an *un*caused beginning ten to twenty billion years ago. This suggests that PSR breaks down at this cosmological level too (as we consider further in the last section of this chapter). The second difficulty is that, physics aside, we must weigh the possibility that the universe is just not the sort of thing to which PSR can apply, because it is just not the sort of thing that can have an explanation. Thus imagine that the universe is the sum total of *all* there is—of everything whatever, without exception—so that there is nothing beyond the universe. An explanation of its existence would still have to be cast in terms of something beyond. (The explanation of one thing is another thing.) Hence there could be no explanation.

In response to this second difficulty, theists are likely to insist that something would have been left out—God—so that there would after all be something beyond the universe. And of course it *is* true that if there is something beyond, there is something beyond in terms of which the universe's existence could have an explanation. If God exists beyond the universe, the universe is the sort of thing that could have an explanation, whereas if God does not exist and there is nothing beyond, the universe apparently is not the sort of thing that could have an explanation. But this implies that PSR would apply to the universe only if God exists, so that theists would be begging the question of whether God exists if they appealed to PSR to show that God exists. Instead they would have to give reasons for believing in God that do not rely on applying PSR to the universe.[4]

In view of all this, PSR seems far more vulnerable than many have supposed. PSR can no longer be used, undefended, as an assumption in various arguments, including arguments for the existence of God. One such theistic argument is the "cosmological" or "first-cause" argument: The universe exists, and exists contingently, but every contingently existing thing has an explanation in the existence and power of something beyond; therefore, there must be some creator, which is God. Only if PSR is adequately defended against the foregoing sort of objection should this cosmological argument persuade. Even then it need not persuade. What, if anything, warrants the assumption that the "something beyond" the universe is one and the same as the God of Scripture?

The fragility of PSR causes problems for some other arguments. One is a popular way of trying to reconcile the theory of evolution with the belief that God created the Earth and human beings much as they are today. The two can be reconciled, many think, by supposing that God created the early conditions out of which we naturally evolved. God brought us about by bringing about conditions long ago that then brought us about.

Unfortunately, this attempt at a reconciliation presupposes that

PSR applies to evolution. The essential features of each stage of evolution are supposed to be determined without remainder by those of the previous stage, so that given the first stage, which God created, we are the inevitable outcome. But according to evolutionary biology, new species, including our own, come about through natural selective pressures that operate on differences generated by random mutations in the genetic material. Because the mutations are genuinely random—genuinely spontaneous or nondeterministic—the essential features of a given stage are *not* determined without remainder by those of the previous stage. From this point of view, our species is here by accident, as are all species; their existence and essential features are by no means completely necessitated by what went before. Nor can PSR be invoked, undefended, to argue that the essential features of each stage *must* be completely determined. PSR cannot be used to argue that the seeming randomness is not in nature but in our lack of knowledge of the relevant factors. Those who would reconcile Biblical accounts of creation with evolutionary biology evidently must find some way of doing so that does not assume evolutionary biology is consistent with the necessitation of each stage by its predecessor.

Theists could of course reply that even if a given stage is not determined by the *natural* features of an earlier stage, it hardly follows that it is not determined by them in conjunction with a supernatural cause. And theists might then postulate some supernatural intervention at each stage of evolution, some divine loading of the dice in favor of those branchings that resulted in us, so that PSR is satisfied after all. But as before, such a move appears strained, artificial, ad hoc, even though it yields a position that is logically consistent. A true reconciliation or synthesis, it seems, would combine evolutionary biology with divine creation without invoking PSR. But whether or how this might be done is another matter.[5]

MYSTERY AND ULTIMATE EXPLANATION

The word 'mystery' is used many ways. Here we will use it, as do most people, in accord with its etymological origins.[6] In this sense a mystery, broadly speaking, is what is expressed by a question to which we do not know the answer, though the question does have a true answer we might some day know (or might not). Defined this way, mysteries run from the trivial to the profound. Toward the trivial end of the spectrum we find, How many paper clips have I used in my life? Toward the profound we encounter questions such as, Does time have a beginning? Thus there can be mysteries aplenty, some of them profound. The issue before us is not whether there are any genuine mysteries but which ones there are or which questions express genuine mystery and which ones seem to but do not.

In this spirit, consider the question, Why does anything at all exist? Sometimes this is called "the question of being," by William James (1842–1910), for example, and later by Heidegger in a different sense. Does the question of being express a mystery? That is, is it a question to which we do not know the answer, though the question does have a true answer we might some day know (or might not)? That depends on what the question is asking. Suppose for now we interpret the question of being as asking for an explanation, so that it means, What is the explanation of why anything at all exists? This is to construe the question as an "explanation-seeking why question." The explanation it seeks is an *ultimate* explanation, meaning that in some sense it is the most profound and far-reaching of all explanations. Later in this section and in the next we consider some other ways of interpreting the question.

Construed as an explanation-seeking why question, the question of being presupposes that *there is* some explanation of why anything at all exists. It presupposes that there is some reason why there is a world "instead of the nonentity which might be imagined in its place," as James put it. If there is no such explanation, the question is based on a false presupposition and is out of order. Asking it would be like asking, What is the way to trisect an angle using only compass and straightedge? There is no true answer to this question, because there is no way to trisect an angle using only the means specified, as we have known since the nineteenth century. Earlier geometers did not know, and they kept searching for a way to do it. For them the question of how to trisect an angle using only compass and straightedge expressed a mystery, though it was one they expected would eventually be solved. But we now know that the question is bogus and can express no mystery. This is not because the question is *meaningless* but because it is based on a false presupposition.

Is there an explanation—known or unknown, knowable or unknowable—of why anything at all exists? Suppose we take this to be asking whether there is some explanation of why the sum total of *all* there is exists. Clearly, if there is some explanation, it is in terms either of something not in the sum total of all there is or of something in the total. But of course there is *nothing* not in the sum total of *all* there is, not even God. The phrase "sum total of all there is" is or purports to be completely comprehensive, referring to everything whatever. So the explanation, if there is one, must be in terms of something in the total—some being or Being or entity or process or realm *X*, not necessarily "determinate." But this means that something about *X*—something in *X*'s nature—not only explains why everything other than *X* exists but also why *X* itself does. That is, *X* would have to be a something (or a somewhat) that exists by a necessity of its own nature. In this sense, *X* would have to be a necessary being.

It follows that if the notion of a necessary being is incoherent, as some philosophers believe, there can be no explanation of why the sum total of all there is exists. The question of why there is anything at all, if construed as an explanation-seeking why question, would be based on a false presupposition and would therefore express no mystery. Asking it would be like asking how to trisect an angle using only compass and straightedge. True, when we hear the words, Why does anything at all exist?, we may find ourselves irresistably feeling a kind of curiosity or a sense of mystery or wonder. But the power of a question to generate a feeling of curiosity or mystery is one thing, and whether the question is based on a false presupposition is another. A question does not cease to have a false presupposition just because we experience a sense of curiosity or wonder when we hear it.

Suppose on the other hand that the notion of a necessary being is *not* incoherent. Could someone then show that the existence of the sum total of all there is does have an explanation in terms of a necessary being? Showing that it has such an explanation would not

But PSR is a necessary
Condition for any rationality whatsoever

be at all easy. We cannot just assume PSR, undefended, in order to
support the presupposition that there must be some explanation or
other. If there need be none, there need be none in terms of a
necessary being. But even if this *could* be shown, the question of
being still would not express a mystery, in all likelihood, let alone an
unsolvable one.

The reason is that we are using the word 'mystery', in accord with
its origins, to mean what is expressed by a question to which we do
not know the answer. In this sense of the term, there would be a
mystery as to why anything at all exists only if no one knew the
answer. But those who promote the notion of a necessary being
typically do so precisely in order to argue that anyone who grasps the
concept of this being as a necessary being will automatically understand why it exists, as we saw early in this chapter: Just as it is of the
essence or nature of a plenum to be full, so is it of the essence or
nature of God to exist. God exists by a necessity of God's own nature.
Anyone who persists in asking Why simply fails to grasp the concept,
either of a plenum or of God. This is how the idea of a necessary
being is supposed to put an end to the regress of why questions.
Consequently, if someone showed us that there is indeed a necessary
being in terms of which (or whom) the sum total of all there is has an
explanation, then in all likelihood we would know why that being
exists (it exists by a necessity of its own nature) and thereby also why
anything at all exists. There would therefore be no mystery, in the
sense intended here, though of course in *other* senses there might well
be plenty of room for the mysterious.

He wants it blocked?

There is only one way this conclusion can be blocked. One would
first have to show that the sum total of all there is does have an
explanation for its existence in some necessary being. But one would
also have to show that those who grasped the concept of this being as
a necessary being would *not* automatically understand why it exists.
This is a narrow loophole indeed. Call it "the loophole of being."
Philosophers must somehow wriggle through it if they want to argue
that the question of being, construed as an explanation-seeking why
question about the sum total of all there is, does express a genuine
mystery. Not that the problem of whether anyone can wriggle through
the loophole of being is the only or the main reason why some

philosophers have not taken the question of being seriously. Rather, this problem is a major obstacle in the way of supposing that the question expresses a genuine mystery.

Suppose no one can wriggle through the loophole of being. Then we must conclude not only that the question of being expresses no mystery in the sense intended here, but we must also conclude that it cannot be used, as often it is used, to argue that certain matters transcend any human capacity to reason about them. The argument is that by reasoning, humans have never been able to solve the mystery of why there is anything at all, rather than nothing. Instead the answer is to be found through mystical insight into some incompletely expressible "beyond."

The trouble with this argument is that the question of why there is anything at all does not express a mystery, in the intended sense, unless someone can show how to negotiate the loophole of being. The point is not that there are no genuine mysteries. There are plenty, some profound and possibly unsolvable. It's just that the question of being seems to many philosophers not to be one of them. It therefore seems to them not to be an occasion for arguing that some matters transcend our reason, though there might be other occasions for arguing this.

So far we have been construing the question of being as an explanation-seeking why question about the sum total of all there is. Suppose instead that when someone asks, Why does anything at all exist?, what is being asked is, What is the *purpose* or *meaning* of it all? Like every question, this one has presuppositions. One is that there *is* some purpose or meaning. If there is none, the question is based on a false presupposition and expresses no mystery; if there is one but we know (or enough of us know) what it is, then again there is no mystery. Another presupposition is that there is only *one* purpose or meaning. If there is *more* than one, then again the question can express no mystery. This could happen if the whole of existence proved to have many meanings or purposes—many ways it is to be "used" or appreciated or respected, many kinds of significance—no one of which excludes or dominates the others or takes some sort of unconditional priority over them.

Sometimes we ask questions not to get an answer but to express an emotion. Why was I ever born? is rarely a request for an account of how one's parents met and of their motives for mating. More often it is a cry of frustration or despair or even the wish to die. Likewise, Why is there anything at all? might be used to express some emotion—despair, perhaps, at the condition of the world, even a despair so great as to be the wish that there had never been anything at all; better that nothing at all should have existed than *this* horror. Or the question might be used to express the opposite, perhaps enchantment at the fact of existence, or affirmation, or astonishment. In each case, so long as the form of the words, Why is there anything at all?, is not being used to express an explanation-seeking why question, there is no mystery expressed in the sense at issue here. Likewise, no such mystery is expressed if the question is used, as it is used by some philosophers, to symbolize the need for wonder or the holiness of a kind of questioning that is never satisfied with dogmatic answers or shopworn accounts.[7]

IS THERE A GROUND OF BEINGS?

There is a further way of construing the question of being. Heidegger claims that the question of why anything at all exists takes priority over all other questions, first, "because it is the most far-reaching, second, because it is the deepest, and finally because it is the most fundamental of all questions."[8] If Heidegger construed the question as an explanation-seeking why question about the sum total of all there is, of course he would encounter the difficulties surveyed above. As we saw, the question would be based on a false presupposition, unless Heidegger could negotiate the loophole of being. But Heidegger attempts no such thing. He does not argue that the existence of the sum total of all there is has an explanation in terms of a necessary being and that nevertheless one who grasped this being's nature or essence still would not know why it exists.

Instead, Heidegger construes the question of why anything at all exists in another way. He construes it as the question of why any-*thing* exists (any entity, being, "essent"). Here the Why asks not for the explanation but for the *ground* of things' existing insofar as they exist ("the ground of what is insofar as it is"). Moreover, the ground is not to be thought of as yet another thing or being, not even as a very special thing or being. "This question 'why' does not look for causes that are of the same kind as the essent itself."[9] Instead, it looks for "being," the ground of beings. Thus the question of why there is anything at all amounts to the question of what is the ground of beings, or simply, What is being? Further, this ground "remains unfindable, almost like nothing."[10] Since the ground, or being, remains thus hidden from us, there is supposed to be genuine, unfathomable mystery here, the mystery of being.

Heidegger's way of taking the question of being differs in important respects from the other ways we have so far considered. Even so, some of the same problems arise. Even if we are to ask, "What is the ground?" rather than "What is the explanation?" there remains the presupposition that *there is* some ground. Must there be one? Is it because everything has a ground? But this principle (Everything has a ground), whether or not Heidegger presupposes it, seems in no better shape than the closely related PSR (Everything has an explanation). And is there such a thing as *the* ground? Why not several? Furthermore, even if there must be just one ground of beings, what is the ground of the ground? Or does asking this simply show that we do not understand the concept of a ground or of being? If so, do we have an analogue of necessary being, in this case something (namely, being) that is grounded in its own nature? But would such a notion of self-grounding even make sense, or is the ground of something always something else? In these ways problems that arise for a relation of explanation may also arise for a notion of grounding. Some philosophers believe there is little in Heidegger to help resolve these problems; some others find him profound.

In any case, Heideggerians are likely to reply that there is far more to the view than this. The question, What is being?, animates the whole of Heidegger's philosophy. His is a philosophy that amounts to one long meditation on the question of being. Minimally, being is something that beings have simply insofar as they exist. Further, Heidegger proposes that in order to ask the question of being, I should begin by asking what my own being is, what it is for me to be.

His answer is that the kind of being that asks, "What is being?" is one who is a *Dasein*, one who is a "being-there," meaning a being-in-the-world, one who inhabits an environment, not as an object or thing and not as a detached ego but as involved with the world and with other human beings. Further, as being-there we are essentially in time, essentially temporal, with a past, present, and future, with projects we care for, and with a sense that death finally will overtake us.

Above all, *Dasein* is to be seen as a kind of bright clearing in a dark forest, a clearing into which beings come from out of the surrounding realm of forest. Beings are not individual things until let into the clearing by us as *Dasein*. The dark surrounding realm sorts itself into realities only by being let into the clearing by us. Only then are there really things. We allow them being, though we do not create them out of thin air. We are "the shepherd of being."

This sketch cannot possibly do justice to the richness and subtlety of Heidegger's view or to the poetic way he often presents it. Nevertheless it does reveal how his view, so far from resolving or clarifying our problems, adds two more, though he might say that it is part of his task to do just that. One problem is whether there is something—being—that all beings have in common simply by virtue of existing. On one interpretation, Heidegger often seems to think that because we say of each existing being that it *is*, and thereby apply the same word 'is' to all beings, therefore beings all share something beyond the fact that they all *are*. This "something" apparently is not quite a *property*, but it does seem to be a feature that amounts to more than merely existing. This further feature beings are supposed to share is that of being. But many philosophers hold that being or existence is neither a property nor a feature nor anything like one. The traditional slogan for their view is, Existence is not a predicate. To say of a thing that it is or exists is only to say that it has or instantiates the properties or the features it does have. On this view, the thing does not have something further, namely being. It just is.

The second problem is that Heidegger's way of construing the question of being requires that you and I begin by asking what our own being is, what it is for us to be. Why begin this way? Why not begin with, say, the being of independently existing things, as we saw the realist begin in Chapter 2? And does beginning with our own being mean it enjoys some unconditional priority over all else? Heidegger's way of approaching the question of being seems to presuppose a form of antirealism, according to which things do not exist independently of us but depend for their existence at least in part on something to do with human being. The question of why there is anything at all is to be answered in terms of how human being-there lets things come into being out of the dark, undifferentiated forest that surrounds the clearing. Though the metaphor is significantly different, we are not that far from talk of a noumenal dough shaped by us into objects. But if this antirealism is false, as many believe, Heidegger's question of being is based on a false presupposition and expresses no mystery. Heideggerians might object that only by way of some such idealism can the reductive and alienating tendencies of realism's preoccupation with objects be overcome. The obvious reply is that realism proper entails no such thing, as we saw in Chapter 2, though there are scarecrows in the neighborhood that do. But this reply may be a bit off the mark, as we see next.

WHAT IS A THING?

A philosopher otherwise as unlike Heidegger as can be imagined has raised the possibility that what we ordinarily call things or objects are mere "projections" onto the world. The world does not really or "objectively" contain things or objects.[11] The idea is that the mind perceives various elements or items as grouped together in certain favored ways rather than in others. It then bestows the title "thing" or "object" on the favored groupings. Research in psychology reveals that the mind uses a number of apparently innate principles to form such groupings and thereby "structures the world into units or unities."

For example, the subject will group a series of circles into two objects on the basis of proximity: OOO OO. The three circles on the left form one object, the two on the right form the other. The subject will not "gerrymander" by taking the left-most four as forming an object or the right-most three or every other one or whatever. Circles that are equally close but different in size will be grouped into objects on the basis of size: ooOOO. The left-most two form one, the right-most three form another. Again subjects will not gerrymander. Other, more complex principles of grouping have been found. They too govern grouping on the basis of various types of similarity, temporal and typal as well as spatial. They amount to strong innate constraints on grouping or perceiving items in certain ways as unities or things. We seem to "entify" by forming a world of entities or things from items or elements in a particular way. Another sort of creature, perhaps from another planet, might group or perceive them very differently.

Indeed, the groupings we form can seem arbitrary. Why not group items in other ways to form other sorts of unities or things? What is so special about *our* scheme? True, the constraints on how we entify evidently are innate, hence not subject to change by learning. But if we *could* change them, why not? Or do the existing constraints on entification somehow correspond to the *right* way of grouping? Even more troubling is the question of whether there *is* a right way of grouping. If there is none, then our way of grouping is a mere projection of our peculiar psychology onto an objectively thingless world. "There is no property of entitivity in the natural world, says the projectivist. It is a mistake to suppose that some things . . . have entitivity while others lack it. It is just a propensity of the mind to interpret the world this way."[12]

It will not do to reply that the items grouped are *themselves* entities or things, as for example are the circles in the preceding illustration. For each circle too is a grouping of items—particles of ink on the page. The same questions can arise about each circle as about the "things" they are grouped together to form. Why not group the ink particles in a different way to form not one circle but *two* things or objects—say, two half circles joined at their tips? Or why not group the particles so that they form *no* object but only *part* of one—perhaps the object that is composed of all the ink particles on this page? We seem not very far from Heidegger here. The particles—or perhaps something beyond them, out of which *they* are grouped—are the forest. Our psychology is the clearing where things or entities come to be. If so, empirical science, in the form of perceptual psychology, seems merely to have caught up, finally, with an insightful philosopher. This is not the first time this sort of thing has happened in the long history of relations between science and philosophy.

Note that the projectivism we are considering here presupposes there is at least one mind-independent item, namely the natural world, which in turn contains some mind-independent items. The only issue is whether these items—the particles or something beyond them—may be grouped in an objectively right way to form objects or things. This position might be called "*naturalistic* projectivism." There are more radical views in the neighborhood, according to which nothing at all is mind-independent, neither the natural world nor even some completely amorphous noumenal dough. Heidegger's view seems to lie somewhere between this radical extreme and naturalistic projectivism.

Before asking how realists might respond to this projectivist account—that is, to *naturalistic* projectivism—recall that we were also wondering whether the question of being expresses a mystery. The answer, on a projectivist account, seems to be no. For some pages now we have been provisionally following Heidegger in construing the question of being as the question of why there is any-thing rather than no-thing. That is, we have been asking why there are any of what we ordinarily call things or objects. But according to projectivism, there are strictly or objectively no such things in the world, though there are some mind-independent, naturally occurring items in the world. Hence the question of why there are any of what we ordinarily call objects, if it is construed as the question of why there are any objectively in the world, is based on a false presupposition and expresses no mystery. On the other hand, suppose the question is why there are any things in the world *as we perceive or interpret it.* Then there is a true answer, but it is one we know, or know well enough. We know the answer, says the projectivist, thanks to recent research in empirical psychology, according to which certain innate principles constrain the mind, or the mind-brain, to group or unify or entify in certain ways rather than others. So again there is no mystery.

How might realists respond to naturalistic projectivism? They might begin by issuing a reminder. Realism does not entail that everything we *think* is real or mind-independent must *be* so (as we saw at the end of Chapter 2). If it turns out that what we ordinarily call things, entities, or objects merely represent the mind's propensity to interpret the world a certain way, so be it. Let them go the way of commonsense simultaneity and determinate position-and-momentum. What *does* have mind-independent existence would then be whatever it is out of which we form the groupings or unities we call objects or things. The "whatever-it-is" might even prove to be quantumstuff, or else the infinitely large, indivisible, dynamic fields physicists talk about. Such stuff and fields have a number of definite properties, described by various equations. Hence they can hardly be called *noumenal* dough or dismissed as a completely dark, undifferentiated forest or as a totally indescribable, ineffable somewhat.

But are realists really able to resist the slide into noumenalism? True, commitment to a noumenal realm is, by itself, consistent with realism. Some realists have indeed held that what alone has real or mind-independent existence is some such realm. Yet it is one thing for realism to be compatible with noumenalism and another to be forced into it. And many would take it as a black mark against realism if it should be forced into noumenalism. This could happen if the same problem arises about the "whatever-it-is" as arises about the things we group together out of it. For example, suppose the "whatever-it-is" proves to be an infinitely large, indivisible, dynamic field. This field seems to be a thing or entity, though an extraordinary one. If so, is the field itself a result of the mind's interpretive activity at work on something beyond?

Realists are likely to object that the notion of "grouping" or "unifying" various items into things or objects presupposes that those further items exist, that they are actually there. If there are no further items—nothing beyond—then the notion breaks down. There is nothing further for the mind to work on or interpret. It made sense to think of the circles as items grouped a certain way to compose things. It also made sense to think of the circles in turn as composed of the ink particles. It even made some sense to think of the ink particles as themselves composed of further items—molecules, perhaps. But at this point we were already straining at the leash. For insofar as we were talking of principles that constrain our natural or unaided *perception*, the items the mind groups or interprets must be perceivable to the unaided senses. Yet the molecules of which the ink particles are composed are not perceivable to the unaided senses.

Suppose we were to waive the requirement that the further items or raw materials the mind is to work on must be perceivable. Still they must at least be there—they must at least exist—in order for the mind to group or interpret them. If they are not—that is, *if there is nothing further*—the notion of grouping or interpretation breaks down. And unless someone can give us reason to believe otherwise, there is nothing further out of which to group or compose the infinitely large, indivisible, dynamic field. Here we seem to reach bedrock in the grouping game.

Another way realists could try to stop the slide into noumenalism is earlier, when the projectivist first claims that there is no property of entitivity in the world because there is no right way of grouping items to compose entities. The projectivist has two arguments for the claim that there is no right way:

First, it is puzzling how there could be any facts in the natural world which would dictate that certain conglomerations of elements have entitivity and other conglomerations lack it. Second, and more centrally . . . we do not need to postulate genuine possession and nonpossession of entitivity in order to explain people's preferences for certain unity schemes (or certain objects) rather than others. Those preferences can be explained much more parsimoniously in terms of innate psychological constraints.[13]

The second argument may prove a red herring. Even if we do not need to postulate genuine entitivity in order to explain people's preferences, we may need to postulate genuine entitivity in order to explain something else, something equally important if not more so.

Indeed realists are likely to take this line. They may begin by emphasizing that naturalistic projectivists themselves presuppose there are facts in the natural world. Naturalistic projectivists question only how such facts could dictate that certain conglomerations of elements in the natural world have entitivity while others lack it. It is the natural world, via natural science, that is the arbiter of what there really or objectively is. Thus naturalistic projectivists are in no position to protest if the concept of an object that realists use is from natural science and from physics in particular.

The key strand of the physicist's concept of an object is invariance. An object is a certain sort of spatiotemporally extended invariant. In particular, not only does it persist through different perspectives or frames of reference. Its existence is what most simply accounts for varying appearances in the different perspectives. When we look at a round dinner plate, most of the time it appears in our visual field as an oval or ellipse, which is also the shape of its image on the retina. Seen edge-on, the plate appears straight. Only when viewed from directly above or below, from a point on the perpendicular to its center, does it appear circular. And only because we already know the plate is circular do we know to view it from some such point if we want the appearance to coincide with the reality. How, then, did we first come to realize that the plate is round? By recognizing that a round thing would present exactly the sequence of shapes we observe, the ellipses that vary from thin to fat. *We accord objecthood or entitivity to whatever would most simply account for or "unify" all these varying appearances.* By postulating a certain sort of object or thing rather than another we inject coherence and simplicity into what would otherwise be an unmanageable plurality or flux of distinct appearances. The physicist's concept of an object obviously has a deep taproot in common sense.

Physics then takes the commonsense concept a step further. Not only does attributing objecthood or entitivity in a certain way provide the simplest account or explanation of the sequence of appearances of the object. It enables us to construct explanations of *other* phenomena—explanations that are simpler and more adequate than any that could be based on gerrymandered "objects." For example, by grouping items in the solar system into sun, planets, moons, and the like rather than into gerrymandered groupings or parts of them, and by subsequently formulating our theories of the solar system in terms of these, we are best able to explain and predict what we observe by way of tides, eclipses, orbital periods, and the rest. When projectivists show how to construct a theory that not only rivals Newton's but adopts a significantly different scheme of entification, we may begin to take projectivism seriously. The fact about the natural world which dictates that certain conglomerations of elements have entitivity and others lack it is the fact that by according certain conglomerations entitivity, we can best explain and predict the phenomena. Or so the realist will argue.

What then is a thing? On the foregoing realist account, a thing or object or entity is a grouping or conglomeration that is a spatio-temporally extended invariant, the postulation of which affords the best explanation of various phenomena. Not only does it explain such phenomena as the varying appearances of the thing. It explains other phenomena as well, such as solar system phenomena or whatever phenomena prove to be relevant in a given case. A scheme or principle of entification that does not meet this standard is to that extent not the right one.

Or at any rate it is not the right one relative to the context naturalistic projectivists themselves operate in when they ask whether a certain concept represents a mere projection onto the natural world. The context in which they operate is one in which natural science is the arbiter of what there really is. Relative to this sort of context, therefore, the right scheme of entification to use is whatever natural science uses. And at least in our century, natural science uses the scheme lately outlined.

To be sure, we human beings often operate in contexts in which we are *not at all interested in explanations*, let alone the explanations characteristic of physics. There is nothing unconditionally prior or fundamental about the physicist's interests. Instead, to consider just one example, we might take an esthetic interest in the world. We might group or perceive its various items or elements in all sorts of novel and gerrymandered ways, perhaps in the manner of Picasso. In *this* sense there need be *no one right way* of grouping, no one way the world is, even though relative to the sort of interest presupposed by the naturalistic projectivist, ironically, there does appear to be one right way of entification.

DOES THE UNIVERSE HAVE A BEGINNING?

If the universe has a beginning, physics assures us, the beginning occurred tens of billions of years ago. If it has an end, the end will come tens of billions of years from now. By any ordinary reckoning, years in the billions amount to an eternity. Why should we care about events so distant in time? If the universe ends, each of us will be long dead and so too will our civilization, our planet, our sun. Meanwhile, there remain the more urgent problems of getting on with our lives. Nor does it matter whether the universe has a beginning, since in any case we find ourselves here, as we are, with all the same problems.

Despite reflections such as these, many people remain fascinated by questions about origins and ends. Simple intellectual curiosity cannot account for their fascination. They imagine a deeper significance. Surely a beginning of the universe means it was created, indeed created by a divine being, for a purpose that concerns us. And surely an end implies something about our fate. Even if we somehow avoid destroying ourselves and our planet, whether by war or pollution, and even if we learn to travel beyond our solar system and survive its inevitable death when the sun turns nova, we cannot survive the death of the universe.

Creation and fate therefore seem to be at stake when theoretical physics takes up first and last events. Yet many believe that questions of creation and fate are beyond the reach of physics and indeed of any science. They belong instead to theology and metaphysics.[14] This is one reason that questions about a beginning of the universe have traditionally been relegated by physics to metaphysics. Another has to do with the situation in physics itself. Until the twentieth century there seemed to be no way of bringing observational evidence to bear on whether and how the universe has a beginning or end. The whole issue was deemed entirely speculative, best left to metaphysicians and theologians.

Traditionally, there were supposed to be only three plausible positions on whether the universe has a beginning. One is that it has none, that it has always existed, that for each moment of time at which it exists there is an earlier such moment. The second is that it was caused to begin at some finite time in the past, before which it did not exist. The third is agnostic: There simply is not enough evidence to say, and perhaps there never will be.

A fourth possibility, that the universe has an *un*caused beginning, was never seriously entertained. For it was held that, necessarily, every beginning has a cause by something else. This causal principle is of course a close relative of PSR. To say that every beginning is caused by something else is to imply that every beginning has an explanation in terms of the causal activity of something else. This is simply a special case of the quite general PSR that everything whatever has an explanation.

Even though the causal principle is less general than PSR, it too conflicts with quantum physics. The creation of a beta particle at a particular instant in the decay of a uranium atom is an uncaused beginning. Though conditions in the nucleus are favorable for the production of beta particles, the conditions do not determine that *this* particle will begin, at *this* instant, even if over a period of time some particle or other must begin.

This does show that there are uncaused beginnings and that the causal principle is wrong (unless someone can show that these seemingly uncaused quantum events have some supernatural or other cause). But it does not at all show (nor is it meant to show) that the *universe* has an uncaused beginning. For by definition the universe contains everything there is or ever was or will be. Thus the beginning of the universe would have to be preceded by nothing whatever. This means there is a crucial disanalogy with the case of the beta particle and similar cases. The beta particle was preceded by the conditions in the nucleus of the uranium atom from which it was emitted, even though it was not caused by them. Whether the universe has an uncaused beginning would have to be settled, if it can be, by appeal to something other than the fact that there are uncaused or spontaneous beginnings *within* it.

Increasingly it looks as though physics might someday settle the issue. Observational evidence that bears on the question of a beginning began to accumulate in the late 1920s. It was observed that light from distant clusters of galaxies is shifted toward the red, just as the sound of a car's horn is Doppler-shifted to a lower pitch as the car moves away from us. The redshift is interpreted to mean that the galactic clusters are all receding from each other, hence that the universe is expanding uniformly in all directions. It's as though they were all hurled outward by some colossal explosion. Further evidence confirms that this is basically what happened. The universe seems to have a beginning ten or twenty billion years ago in a "big bang" out of a superdense, superhot, vanishingly small volume. The very matter of which the galaxies and everything else are composed emerged at or soon after the big bang by natural processes that are increasingly well understood.

This scenario is called "big bang cosmology," and for some years it has enjoyed a consensus among physicists. Some think the big bang is compatible with the universe's being infinitely old. The idea is that after a period of expansion, gravitational forces cause the galactic clusters to contract into a "big crunch," out of which there is another big bang, expansion, contraction, and so on forever. Lately, however, the evidence and argument have been running against an infinitely old oscillating universe.[15]

Suppose we think of the big bang as a genuine beginning of the universe, the first state of the universe, the first state of four-dimensional space-time and its contents.[16] Where does *it* come from? In the 1960s it was shown that any universe that satisfies certain quite general conditions must have a "singularity" in its past, a point (or points) in a space of fewer than four dimensions into which everything is squeezed with infinite density, temperature, and curvature (the Hawking-Penrose singularity theorems). Since a singularity is a point of fewer than four dimensions, it cannot be an *event*, for events are what occur at points in four-dimensional space-time. Instead, a singularity is a boundary or edge of the four-dimensional space-time. Further, a singularity is by definition a point at which a curve in the space-time terminates and at which it is impossible to extend the space-time (for example, because of infinite curvature). This entails that the singularity cannot be preceded by any points in four-dimensional space-time, that is by any events.

The current evidence strongly suggests that our universe satisfies the postulated conditions. If so, there is a singularity in our past, and that is where the big bang comes from. The big bang, the beginning of the universe, is the explosion of four-dimensional space-time out of the singularity. Since the singularity cannot be preceded by any events, the singularity cannot be caused by some earlier natural event or process. What about the big bang? Is it not only preceded but also caused by the singularity? According to the notion of a cause that is relevant here, the singularity would cause the big bang only if it determined the configuration of the particles that constituted the big bang. But the equations used in big bang cosmology, which derive from Einstein's general theory of relativity (GTR), represent the singularity as emitting all configurations with equal likelihood. Thus the singularity does not determine the actual configuration, and the big bang too is uncaused. It looks as though the universe has an uncaused beginning, whether the beginning is identified with the singularity or with the big bang. In either case it spontaneously began to exist. Therefore, it seems contemporary physical cosmology cannot be cited in support of the idea of a divine cause or creator of the universe.

One response to all this is to concede that so far as *physics* goes, the universe does have an uncaused beginning. Nevertheless, there remains a question that is not even touched on by physics or any science: Why does this spontaneously beginning universe exist, why not some other universe or nothing at all? This is our old friend, the question of being, in another form. It asks for the explanation (causal or otherwise) of why this universe exists rather than some other or nothing at all. It therefore presupposes there is some such explanation. But the presupposition is highly vulnerable, as we've seen, in view of the fragility of PSR. Hence the question of being cannot be used, undefended, to insinuate that there must after all be some supernatural explanation or cause of the existence of the universe, something altogether beyond the reach of science. There might be, but we cannot infer that there is on the basis of anything said so far.

Another response is to question the application of GTR to the earliest states of the universe. GTR fails to apply to the conditions of extreme density, temperature, and curvature that obtain during those states. Instead, quantum-mechanical conditions predominate. We need a quantum theory of gravity to guide our thinking about the earliest conditions, but no such theory has yet been adequately developed.

The main problem for this response is that the leading attempts to apply quantum theory to the earliest states represent the universe as spontaneously beginning. One especially intriguing attempt involves "quantum tunneling." According to quantum theory, the energy of a particle multiplied by the time it has that energy is never less than a certain constant magnitude. That is, $\Delta E \cdot \Delta t \nless h/4\pi$, where h is Planck's constant. In conjunction with the rest of the theory, this means that if the time interval Δt is small enough, the energy ΔE becomes spontaneously much greater. An electron that lacks enough energy to cross a barrier may nevertheless cross it by spontaneously acquiring the additional energy during the short interval of time it takes to cross it. The probability that a given electron will in fact tunnel through the barrier in this way can be precisely calculated from the theory. According to prequantum physics it is absolutely impossible for the electron to cross. But quantum theory's prediction of such tunneling has been amply confirmed. There is even observational evidence (though indirect) of the closely related spontaneous emergence of energy or particles in a complete vacuum ("vacuum fluctuation").

Tunneling is normally understood in terms of processes *within* the universe. But *what if we apply the concept to the universe itself,* at that earliest state when it is even smaller than an electron? Since there are no events outside the universe, it looks as though we could speak of the spontaneous emergence of the early universe from nothing. To quote from the abstract of the paper that first advanced this possibility, "A cosmological model is proposed in which the universe is created by quantum tunneling from literally nothing. . . This model does not have a big bang singularity and does not require any initial or boundary conditions."[17] GTR-based big bang models postulate initial states at which the GTR equations themselves break down (because the equations do not apply to the extreme conditions of the initial states). The advantage of the tunneling scenario is that "the structure and evolution of the universe . . . are totally determined by the laws of physics."

May we conclude that nothing in need of explanation has been left out? Not quite. What of the very laws of quantum physics? Why are these fundamental laws true? Surely this needs to be explained, as a number of physicists themselves have suggested.[18] But perhaps it does not need to be explained. Suppose the truth of the fundamental laws is simply a matter of the universe and its contents behaving as the laws say they do. Then the question of why the fundamental laws are true is equivalent to the question of why the universe and its contents behave this way. Like all explanation-seeking why questions, this one presupposes *there is* some explanation. Yet there need be none. PSR is too discredited to guarantee there is one, as is the presence merely of a curiosity feeling. Asking what is the explanation of why the laws of quantum physics are true might be like asking what is the way to trisect an angle using only compass and straightedge.

Suppose that quantum-tunneling accounts of the beginning succeed in dealing with the question of why the fundamental laws are true, either by providing an explanation of why they are true or by showing that the question is based on a false presupposition. There remains a further problem. The beginning, on such accounts, is said to be a tunneling from "literally nothing." But it turns out that the "literally nothing" is not the absolute state of nonexistence theologians have in mind when they speak of creation *ex nihilo.* Instead, "by nothing I mean a state with no classical spacetime."[19] A state with no classical space-time is still a state, even if "it is a rather bizarre state in which all our basic notions of space, time, energy, entropy, etc., lose their meaning." In fact the "nothing" out of which the universe tunnels in this scenario is a space, even though it is not a space-time with all the structure that that implies.

On the other hand, since the space, like the singularity in a GTR–based account, is not preceded by anything, it cannot be caused by some earlier natural event or process. This means that if the *space* is construed as the beginning, instead of the tunneling, it too is an uncaused beginning. Furthermore, there may be a way to rid tunneling accounts of reliance on some preexisting space, however amorphous.[20] If so, space, space-time, and matter are spontaneously born of literally nothing in accordance with the probabilistic laws characteristic of quantum physics. Thus the beginning, though uncaused, would be explained by the laws of quantum physics just as well as any other spontaneous, probabilistic quantum events are explained.

Granted, some of these possibilities are speculative. But they do show that we should look before we leap to embrace the popular belief that the beginning of the universe is something physics can in principle never account for. The popularity of the belief derives in part from the idea that there must ultimately be gaps in what physics and the other sciences can explain. These alleged explanatory gaps are seen as just the places where some supernatural or other nonscientific explanation is called for. For example, theists often invoke God to fill the explanatory gap supposedly left by the inability of physics to explain the beginning. In this way do many people deny science in order to make room for faith.

Unfortunately, belief in a "God-of-the-gaps" is vulnerable to scientific advances that close the gaps. Among the gaps on which theists once relied, and on which many still rely, is the presumed inability of the sciences to explain the origin of the human species or of life or the Earth or our solar system. These gaps have now been largely closed. The ultimate gap, for many theists, concerns the origin of the universe; even if the other gaps are closed, that one can never be. But we have just been seeing how it too might be closed.

The thinking theist, therefore, might consider whether theism really requires a God-of-the-gaps. As some theists themselves have argued, theism properly understood might not be in competition with science over the kinds of explanatory power pursued by the sciences. Perhaps theism is entirely compatible even with the closing by science of every scientific explanatory gap. The trouble with this move is that it is unclear what such a theism would come to. Much of the theist's own talk about God, derived from Scripture, seems inconsistent with complete scientific explainability. Talk of divine miracles, for example, seems to entail the violation or suspension of various physical laws, hence the breakdown of physical explanation. And talk of divine creation seems to entail that the universe was caused to exist, by God. This appears to contradict physical accounts according to which the universe has an uncaused beginning via tunneling from literally nothing. It is not easy to make friends of science and religion.

NOTES

1. *Metaphysics*, 982b13–17.
2. Copleston and Russell (1948), 408.
3. Taylor (1983), 92.
4. A third difficulty is posed by an *a priori* argument against PSR, based on deductive inferences from the very concept of explanation presupposed by PSR, to the effect that not everything can have an explanation of the sort claimed by PSR. Post (1987), secs. 2.3–2.4.
5. Post (1987), 349–353, considers a possible way to do so.
6. Munitz (1965), Ch. 2; Post (1987), sec. 2.1.
7. As in part in Heidegger (1959), Ch. 1.
8. Heidegger (1959), 2.
9. Heidegger (1959), 3.
10. Heidegger (1959), 29.
11. Goldman (1987) raises the possibility—and for him it is apparently only that— mainly in order to show the relevance of cognitive science to metaphysics.
12. Goldman (1987), 543.
13. Goldman (1987), 543.
14. Carroll (1988).
15. Smith (1988), 41–43.
16. Smith (1988), 45–47.
17. Vilenkin (1982).
18. Mortensen (1986), sec. IV, offers a possible explanation.
19. Vilenkin (1983), 2851.
20. Mortensen (1986), sec. III.

5

UNIFYING THE PHENOMENA

THE THALES PROJECT

Aristotle tells us that philosophy begins in wonder. Two centuries earlier, Thales, often said to be the first philosopher, wondered how the world is made, and of what. His answer, "Water," strikes us as charmingly naive. We know so much better. Yet for his day it was a shrewd guess. Water is common, essential to life, and versatile, being the only substance then known to exist in three key forms, liquid, gas, and solid. Positing water as the underlying stuff of which everything is composed therefore had considerable explanatory power and considerable power to unify the phenomena. How the phenomena are, it seemed, is determined by something to do with how water is.

What intrigued Thales' contemporaries and influenced his successors was not his belief that water in particular is the unifying principle. They were excited by the idea that there is an underlying unity, accessible to rational understanding, of which everything else is somehow a manifestation, and a manifestation in such a way that how the underlying stuff is determines how everything else is. Though later philosophers denied that the one stuff is water, they retained the presupposition that despite all differences, everything is a manifestation, not necessarily via composition, of some one kind of existent or some limited variety of kinds, not necessarily kinds of "underlying stuff" or "substance." Many a metaphysician has sought unity in some such limited variety of existents or beings or Being or processes, a unity according to which the properties of these unifiers determine the properties of all the diverse phenomena in which they are manifested. Over the centuries, there have been many candidates for the unifiers. Among philosophers who flourished in just the first century or two after Thales, one finds Anaximander's indefinite, Heraclitus' fire, Parmenides' unchangeable plenum, Democritus' atoms and the void, Pythagoras' numbers, Plato's Forms, and Aristotle's matter and substance plus its movers. Among later philosophers one encounters Descartes' (1596–1650) two substances (mental and physical); Spinoza's (1632–1677) one substance (God-or-Nature); Hegel's (1770–1831) Spirit; Whitehead's actual occasions of becoming; and so on and on.

Each of these philosophical answers to Thales' question amounts to a theory of being *qua* being. Each implies that to be is to be made or composed of or identical with or in some other fashion a manifestation of the unifiers, in such a way that how the unifiers are determines how everything else is. Some imply further that to be is to be *only* or *nothing but* some such affair. Even those that do not imply this mostly assume that the unifiers enjoy an unconditional priority over the mere phenomena that are their manifestations. Discourse about the unifiers is supposed to be privileged over all other discourse and to express *the* way things really are, the dominant pattern of being, the ultimate character of the world. The vocabulary of the privileged discourse is a "final vocabulary."[1]

The fact that so many varieties of metaphysics have been totalizing or monopolistic in these ways can make it look as though *all* varieties *must* be. But we saw in Chapters 1 and 2 that not every theory of being *qua* being need be totalizing or committed to some "final vocabulary." Nor need there be such a thing as *the* way things are, despite the contrary tendency in traditional metaphysics. Here we need to deepen the argument, by looking at an especially relevant contemporary answer to Thales' question. This is the *physicalist* answer: To be is to be composed of the entities physics studies, and how all the phenomena are is determined by the properties of the basic physical entities. Physicalism is widely supposed to be the paradigm of a totalizing or monopolistic metaphysics. In this chapter and the next, we find reason to wonder whether it really is, in contrast with neighboring scarecrows. The lessons we learn in this way about physicalism will turn out to apply to *non*physicalist varieties of metaphysics as well. Whatever the fate of physicalism, therefore, we have ample reason to study it for what it can tell us about metaphysics in general.

A physicalist answer to Thales' question, some philosophers think, is supported by current scientific theory. They are encouraged in this belief by several considerations, including the judgments of some physicists themselves. One physicist even goes so far as to claim that "science has solved the Thales problem . . . at least in the sense it was originally posed."² In the sense it was originally posed, we are told, the problem was about "the structure and composition of bulk matter, by which is meant the objects and substances we find around us," the everyday furniture of the world. The Thales project, which "has remained close to the center of interest of physicists for almost 2500 years," is to find an adequate and observationally testable answer to the problem. The answer, we now know, is that the objects and substances we find around us are composed of particles and processes that the laws of contemporary physics are about (basically the laws of quantum mechanics and of the theory of relativity). Light, heat, color, hardness, the shining of the sun, the behavior of liquids, gases, and solids, all of chemistry, even life—all these and more can be accounted for in this way. Underlying the complexities of the everyday or manifest phenomena is a unifying simplicity described by physics.

This way of construing Thales' question restricts its scope to the everyday phenomena. Metaphysicians are among those who widen the scope. The question is to be construed as about not only what we find around us, but everything whatever, including the basic entities and processes posited by physics itself. What are *they* composed or grouped of? Where do *they* come from? What explains why they follow the laws they do? Of course these further questions might be based on a false presupposition, a possibility we noted in the last chapter. But even if they are, they make us wonder: In order to see the Thales project as having been completed in contemporary physics, mustn't we significantly narrow the project's scope? When we ask not only about bulk matter and everyday processes but about everything whatever, isn't physics bound to fall short?

There are philosophers who disagree. They believe that whatever requires accounting for is adequately accounted for in terms of the basic entities and processes physics investigates. Even when the Thales project is accorded the widest scope, a physicalist answer suffices. Such an answer amounts to a theory of being *qua* being. To be is to be composed of basic physical entities and processes, and in such a way that all the aspects or properties of things are determined by the physical properties of the basic entities and processes. Physicalism is a descendant of the materialism of Democritus, who held that to be is to be a collection of atoms in the void.

Appalling though physicalism is to many people, we need to understand why in our day it is so attractive to others. One reason is that, right or wrong, physicalism is clearly an answer to Thales' question, whether construed narrowly or broadly; some varieties of metaphysics are not. Another reason is that physicalism seems to be supported by the growing success of the sciences in closing explanatory gaps in our understanding of the world. A third is that, unlike some varieties of metaphysics, physicalism does at least address the problem of how to give a plausible account of the relation between scientific and other sorts of truth, a challenge for all varieties of metaphysics we noted in Chapter 1. A fourth reason is that, unlike most other theories of being *qua* being, physicalism is meant to be criticizable by way of observational testing. According to contemporary physicalists, the principles of physicalism are to be treated as high-level empirical hypotheses or generalizations. In this respect they resemble the very abstract and comprehensive principles of theoretical physics. If phenomena turn up that resist a physicalist account even after years of trying, the physicalist's own principles should be rejected or revised. Physicalists are therefore prepared to concede, if need be, that there are more things in heaven and earth than are dreamt of in their philosophy. Or so we are told.[3]

NONREDUCTIVE UNIFICATIONS

Are there more things than are dreamt of in physicalism? It certainly seems so. Our thoughts and feelings, for example, seem anything but merely physical, and it likewise seems impossible to explain in purely physical terms what it is like to be the persons we are, experiencing all that we do. So too for much else. A physicalist unification of everything therefore strikes many as simplistic if not absurd.

How might physicalists respond? They might begin by reminding everyone that a theory of being *qua* being need not be committed to essentialism. According to the physicalist's theory of being *qua* being, to be is to be composed of, or at least realized in, certain basic physical entities or processes. This does not entail that to be is to be *necessarily* or *essentially* thus composed or realized. Our old friend of unforgettable name—Jones—could be composed of or realized in the physical entities that make up Jones's body, but not essentially or intrinsically so. There could be possible worlds—logically or meta-physically possible worlds—in which Jones exists without being thus physically embodied. According to some physicalists, there could even be *physically* possible worlds like this. Suppose, as do many philosophers, that a physically possible world is one in which the only requirement is that the entities in it obey the laws of physics. Then a physically possible world could contain *non*physical entities, so long as they obey the laws of physics. Jones could be made of such entities. Even though physicalism entails that in *this* world Jones is composed of or realized in basic physical entities, and in that sense is a physical thing, it does not entail—and some versions emphatically deny— that Jones is *essentially* or *intrinsically* a physical thing.

But doesn't physicalism entail that everything is *nothing but* a physical thing? Not if saying that Jones is nothing but a physical thing implies that Jones is *essentially* a physical thing. For there are anti-essentialist versions of physicalism. Indeed some versions explicitly reject the "nothing-but" thesis. The point is quite general: According to any theory whatever of being *qua* being, to be is to be such-and-such, but this does not entail that to be is to be *nothing but* such-and-such.

However, the phrase 'nothing but' is often used in another sense. In this sense, to say that something is nothing but a physical thing is to say that all its properties really are equivalent to physical properties, as for example the property of being a middle-A sound is equivalent to being an oscillation in air pressure at 440 Hz or being red is equivalent to having a certain triplet of electromagnetic reflectance efficiencies or being warm is equivalent to having a certain mean level of microscopically embodied energies.[4] A thing need have none of its properties essentially, but all those it does have (or can have) are equivalent to physical properties. Even those of its genuine properties that do not *seem* equivalent to the physical—the property of consciously intending something, for example—really are, in the sense that they can be *reduced* to physical properties. Or so we are told by *reductive* varieties of physicalism, according to which all properties of things are reducible to physical properties. In general, reductive theories of being *qua* being, physicalist or otherwise, do entail that to be is to be nothing but such-and-such.

To reduce one kind of talk about or description of things to another is to show that they are equivalent in some appropriate sense.[5] A nonphysical description—such as 'is thinking'—is equivalent to some physical description—of the brain, say—if they are either necessarily or at least actually true of all the same things. And a nonphysical property—a mental property, for example—is equivalent to some physical property, if necessarily whenever something has one property it has the other. Thus it might happen that the property of my having a sensation of red and the property of there occurring a spiking frequency of 90 Hz in my gamma network[6] are such that whenever something has one it has the other, and has it of necessity, in the sense of according with the laws of some appropriate theory that connects the two kinds of properties.

Until recently it was taken for granted that physicalism must be reductive. Physicalism was supposed to account for everything, if it could, by reducing all things and their properties to purely physical things and their properties. Anything that could not be reduced was supposed to be eliminated as not real, a figment of tender-minded ways of thinking and talking. Perhaps the most notorious reductivist school was the Unity of Science movement within logical positivism, according to which the sciences were to be unified by reducing them all to physics. But the reductivist program, even in its more moderate versions, is widely believed to have failed. True, many important nonphysical properties have proved reducible to some physical property or complex combination of physical properties. Many have not. Indeed, they still resist reduction, even according to some physicalists.

There have been three main reactions to this situation. One is to concede the irreducibility of much talk about minds, thoughts, intentions, and the rest but to conclude that such talk is therefore false or meaningless or otherwise defective, the residue of "folk psychology" or other outmoded ways of thinking. Because such talk cannot be smoothly integrated with an objectively correct picture of the world, it should be eliminated. There really are no minds, thoughts, intentions, or beliefs. This is *eliminative* physicalism, or eliminativism. It presupposes the reductivist's Procrustean principle that whatever cannot be reduced to the physical is to be rejected as not real, and talk about it is to be regarded as fundamentally defective.

A second reaction is to conclude, So much the worse for physicalism: Any view compelled to reject or belittle so much of what is obviously real and important can hardly be taken seriously. This is antiphysicalism, the instinctive first reaction of most people when confronted with these issues.

But there is a third reaction, developed in just the last few years. This is *nonreductive* physicalism: Everything can be accounted for in terms of the physical properties of the underlying entities and processes without having to be reducible to them. Eliminativists and antiphysicalists have so far mostly overlooked this third possibility. A nonreductive physicalism is free to reject not only essentialism but also the view that everything is nothing but a physical thing. Not all the properties of a thing need be reducible or equivalent to physical properties, and many of them seem not to be. In particular, many of the properties in virtue of which we are human beings seem to be irreducible to physical properties or even to complex combinations of physical properties.

It follows that a person or thing can have many kinds of properties that are irreducibly different, properties that are not in any relevant sense equivalent. Not only can things have the physical and other properties studied by the natural sciences or their equivalents. Things can also have properties not equivalent to any physical properties,

including certain mental, intentional, cultural, and historical properties, to mention only a few. Some physicalists even argue that there
are moral and other normative properties that things objectively have.
Nonreductive physicalism is therefore congenial with a thoroughgo-
ing pluralism as regards kinds of properties, even though it affirms a
monism of underlying entities and processes. The monism comes of
asserting that every concrete thing or process is composed of the
basic physical entities and processes. The pluralism enters when the
concrete thing is allowed to have a variety of physically irreducible
properties, even though which of these properties the thing has is
determined ultimately by how things are at the level of the physical
entities and processes. In the next section we explore in more detail
just how this could be.

A thing's properties are or represent the ways it is. Thus on a
nonreductive physicalist account, there is no such thing as *the* way
the thing is or some one kind of property to which all its other
properties can or ought to be reduced. To be is to be composed of or
realized in basic physical entities or processes, but to be is *not* to be
only that. Nor need a thing's own physical properties be accorded
some unconditional privilege or priority. One reason is that the
physical properties the thing has may not be enough by themselves to
account for the nonphysical properties it has. The account may need
to include the physical properties of *other* things, as we see later in
this chapter and the next. The thing may have some of its properties
only in virtue of how things are in a wider environment.

Indeed, the thing may have certain properties only in virtue of the
properties of items separated from it not only in space but also in
time. A *history* is needed, as we saw in connection with Millikan's
theory of proper function, aboutness, and reference. If Millikan is
right, any adequate account of the property of being about or referring to something must be a historical account. The same is likely to
be true of what is called the *intentionality* of an act or thought, since
its intentionality, or its having an intentional property, is largely a
matter of its being about or directed upon something. If Millikan is
right about intentionality, the physical properties that would enter
into the account must include physical properties of things at some

distance in space and time from whatever has the intentional properties (as we see further in the next chapter). If nonreductive physicalism is to be compatible with this determination by physical properties
at a distance in space and time, as it claims to be, it must allow that a
thing's own physical properties often are not enough to account for its
nonphysical properties. So too must any other metaphysics make
room for the distant and the historical.

Some philosophers might be willing to grant that nonreductive
physicalism does not accord unconditional priority to a thing's own
physical properties. Still, doesn't it accord unconditional priority to
the physical properties of all those things, however distant in space
and time, that do enter the account? Not necessarily. A physicalist
might respond as we imagined the realist responding in Chapter 2:
Whatever priority the physical entities and properties may have is
highly *conditional*. *If*, in a given context, we are interested in a
certain kind of account or unification of the phenomena, *then* the
physical entities and properties enjoy a certain priority—provided,
of course, they afford a successful account of this kind; if some
nonphysical entities and properties afford a better such account, they
enjoy this priority. In the context of the Thales problem, for example,
we are interested in finding some kind of being or beings or processes
of which everything is not only a manifestation, but a manifestation in
such a way that how the unifiers are determines how everything else is
and in that sense accounts for and unifies the phenomena. On such
occasions the unifiers—physical or otherwise—that afford the best
such account take on a corresponding sort of priority, perhaps some
kind of explanatory priority.

On others they do not. We often operate in contexts in which we are
not at all interested in explanations, let alone the kind or kinds of
explanation relevant to the Thales problem. We might take an esthetic
interest in the world, grouping or unifying things in ways that have
nothing to do with explanation and determination. On such occasions
various esthetic properties would take priority, evidently some kind
of esthetic priority.

Likewise, when we must take urgent practical action, what take
priority are the manifest aspects of things that bear immediately on

what is to be done. In our life-world what we see is a child in danger, not a collection of basic physical entities, and we pull her to safety. In our life-world, what we do is hug a friend, make a call, hit the brakes, grab a weapon. Our reflexes are keyed to these aspects of things, which take on a corresponding priority. The physicalist could even argue that there is no such thing as unconditional priority. There is only priority-in-a-respect, in a certain context, relative to some interest. We remain free to be interested in other matters.

There is a variety of metaphysics called a "double-aspect theory," descended from Spinoza, according to which the mental and the physical are merely aspects of an underlying substance that is itself neither mental nor physical. Neither aspect is in any sense prior or basic. The underlying substance is what is basic, and it cannot be characterized by any description (although Spinoza himself thought otherwise). In this sense, the "underlying somewhat" is unknowable, a noumenon. Generalizing, we can imagine a "*plural*-aspect" theory, in which the aspects of the "underlying somewhat" are many more than two.

Nonreductive physicalists likewise can talk of a pluralism of aspects or properties, none of which is prior or basic. This sounds like a plural-aspect theory.[7] But there are at least three fundamental differences. First, physicalism posits no unknowable underlying somewhat. The underlying entities and processes that compose things and account for their multiple aspects are supposed to be those we know about from physics. Second, physics does thereby provide a description of how things in the world actually are. They actually are moved and changed by various physical forces, actually have mass-energy, and so on, although there are also *other* ways things actually are. Many things are also conscious, have intentions, deserve to be treated as moral beings, and more (as we see further in the next chapter). Third, there are senses in which one aspect or another *is* prior or basic, though not unconditionally so. For example, consider the context in which Spinoza himself seems to have been working, at least in part, namely the context of finding a theory of being *qua* being that solves the Thales problem. In this context, the basic or underlying aspect of things is the physical, according to physicalism.

In this context, not all aspects are equal, contrary to a plural-aspect theory, and one of them—the physical—affords an important kind of unification of the phenomena.

The physicalist could even argue that there is no one way to unify the phenomena but many—many equally privileged unifications, many ways of seeing things whole. It is only when we are interested in a certain sort of unification that the physicalist's unification is supposed to take priority. Thus assume again that we are working in a context in which we are trying to construct a theory of being *qua* being that answers Thales' question broadly construed and that does so objectively, in an observationally testable way. In such a context, a physicalist unification takes priority, though only if it affords the best such answer.

In other contexts, when we are interested in other things, other sorts of unity are more important. For example, one way things might form a unity is by being objects of our thought or by having a certain significance, value, or meaning for us or by being related to us in some other way or simply by being in space-time. Each of these is or suggests a scheme of unification. Some are suitable for certain purposes, others for others, like different kinds of maps of the same terrain. There are road maps, river maps, topographical maps, maps of mineral deposits and other resources, maps that use unconventional coordinate schemes. Each is deeply compatible with all the others.[8] So too is the physicalist's map compatible even with a map of everything in polar coordinates centered on us. Such an anthropocentric map is no less a map than any other, no less inclusive, no less accurate, no less a way of giving a unified overview of the terrain. It is even preferable for certain purposes, much as earth-centered astronomy is preferable for navigation at sea, though for other purposes we know that a centerless astronomy is the right one to use.

These, then, are some of the ways in which physicalism need not be totalizing or monopolistic. So too for a number of other, *non*physical theories of being *qua* being. Like physicalism, these other varieties of metaphysics need not entail that to be such-and-such is to be *essentially* or *only* or *nothing but* such-and-such. So far from being necessarily reductive or eliminative, they can accommodate not only an irreducible plurality of ways the world is and of its aspects or properties, historical and relational, but also an irreducible plurality of kinds of unity. Nor need such theories accord unconditional priority to any of these. And yet . . .

NONREDUCTIVE DETERMINATION?

Trouble lurks in this warm paradise of pluralism and tolerance. Once again physicalism provides an instructive example. The physicalist claims to be able to account for everything whatever in terms of the basic physical entities, perhaps quantumstuff and curved space-time. *Just how does this account go*, if not by way of reduction to the basic physical things and properties? What *is* the relation between the physical properties and the nonphysical, if not reducibility? What *positive* account can be given, if any? In connection with intentionality, for example, it is not enough for a nonreductive physicalism to be *compatible* with the historical and relational matters involved. Nonreductive physicalists need to give an account of how intentionality arises or emerges from purely physical processes, however distant in space and time. They need to give an account of how the *burden of proof* intentional properties of an act or thought are thereby determined by how things are at the level of physics. Until they do, we are entitled to some skepticism about the physicalist's claim to be able to account for all that needs accounting for.

How have nonreductive physicalists responded to this challenge? To begin with, the relation between the physical properties and the nonphysical, they say, is *nonreductive determination* (also called "supervenience," or a variety of it). The basic idea is simple enough. In everyday language, when we say that one state of affairs determines another, we mean that how the first is settles or fixes how the second can be. Given the way the first is, there is one and only one way the second can be. For example, suppose someone says, rightly or wrongly, that the outcome of a certain battle was determined by the terrain and the commanders' initial disposition of their forces. What is meant is that given the terrain and disposition of forces, there could have been one and only one outcome (as when Hannibal trapped the Romans at Lake Trasimeno).

This is equivalent to saying that given the terrain and disposition of

forces and given any other battle with the same terrain and disposition of forces, the two battles would have the same outcome. To put it
another way, consider any two physically possible worlds in each of
which there is a battle that has the same terrain and disposition of
forces. Then in those worlds the outcome of the two battles is also the
same.

To take a further example, suppose someone says, rightly or
wrongly, that the biological behavior of a cell is determined by the
physicochemical properties of its molecules. This is equivalent to
saying that given two worlds in each of which there is a cell whose
molecules have the same physicochemical properties, the biological
behavior of the two cells is also the same.

These examples suggest an account or explication of what nonreductive physicalists mean when they say that the world's physical
properties determine its nonphysical properties and relations:

D1—Given any two physically possible worlds $W1$ and $W2$, and given any
two things x and y, if x has the same physical properties in $W1$ as y has in
$W2$, then x has the same nonphysical properties in $W1$ as y has in $W2$,

where to say that x has the same physical (or other) properties in $W1$
as y has in $W2$ is to say that for every such property, x has it in $W1$ if
and only if y has it in $W2$. (Also we assume that $W1 \neq W2$ and
$x \neq y$.) For example, to say that the physical properties of a cell's
molecules determine its biological properties is to say that given any
two cells, if their molecules have the same physical properties in $W1$
and $W2$, then the two cells behave biologically the same way in $W1$
and $W2$.

Principle D1 is a mouthful. Sometimes it is abbreviated by saying
that two worlds indiscernible as regards the physical properties of
things in them are indiscernible as regards the things' nonphysical
properties. More briefly still, sometimes one says that the physical
properties determine the nonphysical if and only if physical indiscernibility entails nonphysical indiscernibility; worlds that are physical duplicates are nonphysical duplicates. But beware. Philosophers
often use these shorter ways of putting the matter to abbreviate

principles that sound the same but are significantly different (as we see later in this chapter at D2).

Wariness is in order in another way. *Explication D1 may not quite capture what physicalists and other metaphysicians mean when they talk of determination,* as we begin to see in a moment. Indeed, we will later be compelled to *replace* D1 with a better explication, D2.

Niceties of explication aside, doesn't talk of determination, and in particular of determination of outcomes and behavior, imply determin*ism*? That is, doesn't talk of determination imply that given the state of things at one time, there is one and only one outcome they can have at a later time? And isn't this incompatible with quantum indeterminacy? Physicalists are likely to reply that yes, such universal determinism would indeed conflict with what we know about the world from quantum physics. But talk of determin*ation* does not imply or presuppose determin*ism* Consider the assertion that the biological behavior of the cell is determined by the physical properties of its molecules. True or not, this asserts only that given the physical state of its molecules at a time t, there is one and only one biological state the cell can be in at that same time. It does not follow that given either the physical or the biological state of the cell at t, there is one and only one such state it can be in at a *later* time $t + 1$. Determin*ation* of one kind of state by another is compatible with complete indetermin*ism* as regards how each state evolves through time. Metaphysicians of all stripes, not just physicalists, can therefore talk of determination without landing in determinism.

Connective Generalizations
A more serious problem is *whether determination can really be nonreductive.* Here we are at the frontier of current debate. Like most frontiers, this one can get wild and woolly. Much is new and little is settled over just what the relevant determination relation is (or determination relations are) and whether determination can really be nonreductive (and in what senses). Complications abound, and it may be some time before the forces of law and order tame this frontier to the point where greenhorns can easily understand the territory. But we need to try, not only because the fate of physicalism may depend

on whether determination can be nonreductive but also because *any* metaphysics that aims to be nonreductive has a considerable stake in the outcome.

Some excellent philosophers think determination cannot be nonreductive. They argue as follows. Suppose, rightly or wrongly, that a cell's biological properties are determined by the physical properties of its molecules. Then for each biological property N the cell has— that is, for each N realized by the cell—there must be some possibly complex physical property the molecules have that is equivalent to N. Why? Part of the reason, we are told, is that given such determination of the biological by the physical, then for each realized N there must be a physical property P such that whatever has P also has N.[9] For if the biological is determined by the physical, there should be some explanation of why it is. The only plausible sort of explanation in sight, the argument continues, is one that presupposes there are certain connections between the biological properties and the physical properties. These are connections of the form, Whatever has P also has N.[10] Call such connections *"connective generalizations."*

How might defenders of nonreductive determination respond? They might begin by arguing that determination in the sense of D1 does not entail that for each realized nonphysical property N there is some physical property P such that whatever has P has N. For one can construct a *counterexample* against the claim that determination in the sense of D1 entails the connective generalization. That is, one can construct an example in which determination in the sense of D1 holds, but the connective generalization, Whatever has P has N, does not. Because the counterexample is abstract and its precise force is not easy to see, it helps to begin with the fable of the College and the Old Grad.

Old Grad, now wealthy and a bit eccentric, decides to double alma mater's endowment. In return, the College is to construct two buildings, *B1* and *B2*, to be named after Old Grad's children and to house a new program dear to Old Grad. To ensure efficient use of the new facilities, Old Grad stipulates, the College is to require that for any two students x and y who are qualified for the program, if x takes the same basic courses in *B1* as y takes in *B2*, then x takes the same advanced courses in *B1* as *y* takes in *B2*. (Compare D1: If *x* has the same physical properties in *W1* as *y* has in *W2*, then *x* has the same nonphysical properties in *W1* as *y* has in *W2*.) That is, if students *x* and *y* are the same as regards the basic courses they take in the buildings, then they are to be the same as regards their advanced courses. The College quickly accepts and announces the new policy.

Unfortunately, in the first year of the new program only two students, Smith and Jones, are qualified. They differ in the courses they've already taken, and not all the needed classrooms and labs in the two buildings have been completed. This forces the College to assign courses so that in *B1*, Smith and Jones both take the same basic course and Smith but not Jones takes advanced; in *B2*, Smith but not Jones takes a basic and neither takes an advanced. This means that not everyone who takes a basic in one of the buildings takes an advanced there too, since in *B1* Jones takes a basic but not an advanced, and so too for Smith in *B2*.

Old Grad is upset, having thought the policy entails the generalization that any student who takes a basic in one of the buildings takes an advanced there too. Old Grad hauls the College into court. But the court rules for the College: The assignment of courses to Smith and Jones is consistent with the stipulated policy, even though it is inconsistent with the generalization that whoever takes a basic course in one of the buildings takes an advanced there too. The assignment is consistent with the policy because even though Smith and Jones are not the same as regards the basic courses they take in the buildings (Smith taking a basic in *B1* while Jones does not take a basic in *B2*), nevertheless the College can sincerely claim that *were* they the same in this regard they would be the same as regards the advanced, which is all the policy requires.

Now let's take on the abstract counterexample against the claim that determination in the sense of D1 entails that for each realized *N* there is some physical *P* such that whatever has *P* has *N*. The counterexample parallels the fable. Let there be two worlds *W1* and *W2*, two objects *x* and *y*, one *P*-property *P'*, and one *N*-property *N'*. (The parallel here is to supposing that there are two buildings *B1* and *B2*, two students Smith and Jones, the property of taking a basic course and the property of taking an advanced course.) Suppose further that in $W1$, x and y both have P', and x but not y has N'; and that in $W2$, x but not y has P', and neither has N'. (The parallel here is to supposing that in $B1$, Smith and Jones both take the same basic courses and Smith but not Jones takes advanced, while in $B2$, Smith but not Jones takes a basic and neither takes an advanced.) This example is consistent with D1 but inconsistent with the connective generalization (just as the College's assignment of courses is consistent with Old Grad's stipulated policy but inconsistent with the generalization that whoever takes a basic in one of the buildings takes an advanced there too). Since the only physical property here is P', there is no P such that whatever has P has N'. For even though x and y have the same P-properties in $W1$, y has P' but not N' in $W1$ and so too for x in $W2$.[11]

While we're at it, we can modify this abstract counterexample to show that determination does not entail essentialism. The particulars of the new counterexample are just as before, except that we add a world $W3$ in which neither x nor y has P' and both have N'. This is consistent with a thing's P-properties' determining its N-properties in worlds $W1–W3$. For in any two of these worlds, if x and y are the same as regards whether they have P', they are also the same as regards whether they have N'. Yet neither x nor y has either P' or N' essentially. For in each case there is a world in which the individual does not have the property (and one in which it does). Therefore the individual does not have the property necessarily, hence not essentially.

Dependency, Bruteness, Evidence

Those who find nonreductive physicalism problematic are likely to reply that the counterexamples only show something about a certain *explication* of determination, namely D1. In particular, they show only that the explication fails to entail connective generalizations such as Whatever has P has N. So much the worse for the explication. Determination properly so-called is a relation according to which the nonphysical properties *depend* on the physical properties, and such dependency requires at least that for each realized nonphysical property N there is a physical property P such that whatever has P has N. Any explication of determinational dependency that fails to entail some such generalization is therefore not a good explication.[12]

How might nonreductive determinationists respond? Part of what they are claiming is precisely that there is a relation of dependency that does *not* require the connective generalizations. To demand of any adequate explication of dependency or determination that it entail connective generalizations begs the question of whether there is such a relation. What reason is there to suppose that any relation of dependency or determination between properties must involve connections between them according to which whatever has one has the other?

The reason, one reply goes, is that without the connective generalizations, a claim of determination or dependency would be difficult to understand. There would be no explanation of why or how it happens that the nonphysical properties of a thing are determined by or dependent on its physical properties. Why and how is it that the properties of a cell are determined by certain physical properties? Unless we can answer this question, it would be "a brute and unexplainable . . . primitive fact about the world" that the one kind of property determines the other. Furthermore, if there is no such explanation, what *evidence* could we ever have to support the claim of determination or dependency?[13] If we do not have evidence that whatever has the relevant physical properties P also has N, what evidence *could* we have that the P-properties determine the N-properties? Suppose there is evidence that the physical properties of the molecules in a cell determine its biological properties. How could this not also be evidence that for each biological property N the cell has, it has some complex physical property P such that whatever has P has N?

Nonreductive determinationists might respond by asking why we should not *also* require an explanation for why and how it happens that whatever has P has N. Why the double standard? After all, the connective generalization that whatever has P has N, like the claim that one determines the other, expresses a kind of *correlation*, or dependent variation, between P and N. If we require an explanation of why and how it happens that the *determination* correlation obtains between P and N, why not also for the *generalization* correlation? What exactly is the relevant difference between the two sorts of correlations, if any, in virtue of which one allegedly requires explanation and the other does not?

For example, suppose we discover that whatever has a certain physical property has a certain biological property. What explains this? Or are we entitled to rule this question out of order on the ground that there need be no such explanation? If so, wouldn't it be "a brute and unexplainable . . . primitive fact about the world" that whatever has the physical property has the biological property? If this bruteness would be objectionable in the case of determination, why not also in the case of generalization? In any event, early in Chapter 6, in connection with intentionality, we see how the non-reductive determinationist might argue that often there *is* an explanation of how and why the P-properties determine the N-properties, even though there is no explanation of this based on connective generalizations from P to N.[14]

As for the question of evidence, there are at least two kinds of evidence for the determination of one state of affairs by another.[15] One is observational. We may observe repeatedly that two cells that are the same in relevant physical respects are the same in some given biological respect. Or two masses of gas exactly alike in some relevant respect of the kinetic properties of their molecules may be observed repeatedly to be alike in some given respect of their temperature, pressure, or diffusion rate. Or two organisms alike in relevant neurological respects may be observed always to be alike as regards their learning ability. We can observe such determination correlations even if we know of no explanation for why or how they obtain.

Nor need the observational evidence for these determination correlations be or include evidence for the connective generalization that whatever has a certain property P has a given property N. For the generalization is not entailed by the correlation. Indeed, the observational evidence might well include cases like the Old Grad counterexample, which would imply the falsity of the generalization. In the Old

Grad example, we could gather observational evidence for what the College policy is by observing what classes the students go to each day. This would be evidence for a determination correlation, because, as we have seen, the policy amounts to such a correlation. But it would also be evidence against the generalization that any student who takes a basic course in one of the buildings takes an advanced there too, since we would observe Jones taking a basic in *B1* but not an advanced and likewise for Smith in *B2*. We encounter what is arguably an actual case to the same effect (the Ammon case) later in this chapter.

A second and more important kind of evidence for determination comes in the form of *connective theories*—theories that connect one kind of phenomena with another. Connective theories usually grow out of attempts to unify and systematize the otherwise miscellaneous observed correlations between the two kinds of phenomena. Investigators develop a molecular biology, a quantum-physical chemistry, a kinetic theory of gases, a physiological psychology. An important kind of evidence for such a theory is that it has a certain comprehensiveness and explanatory power, or "consilience." One theory is more *consilient* than another, with respect to accounting for given phenomena N, if it explains more classes or kinds of the N-phenomena. A theory in molecular biology is more consilient than its competitors, hence has more evidence in its favor, if it explains more kinds of biological phenomena than they do.

Thus a connective theory can be and typically is supported by a variety of indirect evidence—evidence other than observations of correlations—though the theory will normally enjoy support from the latter as well. In the fable of the College and the Old Grad, this is like having evidence, other than observation of where the students actually go each day, for what the College's policy is. Furthermore, connective theories often entail not only that a given kind or class of N-phenomena is determined by some underlying P-phenomena. They often entail as well that there is no P-property P such that whatever has P has a given N-property N (as we soon see in the Ammon case below and in Millikan's connective theory of intentionality in Chapter 6). Thus connective *theories* often contain no connective *generalizations*. In this way we can have evidence that the *P*-properties determine the *N*-properties, even though we have no evidence for (and indeed some against) the connective generalization that whatever has *P* has *N*. Or so the nonreductive determinationist will try to argue.

Determination via History

Evidential problems aside, there is another difficulty for nonreductive determination, at least when determination is taken in the sense of D1. Let us say that two items are physically *indiscernible* when there is no physical property one has that the other lacks. And let the physical properties here be only the nonrelational physical properties; we will consider the case of the relational ones in the next section. Now D1 is consistent with there being in one and the same world, perhaps in ours, two items *x* and *y* that are physically indiscernible and yet have different nonphysical properties. This is shown by the abstract counterexample described earlier. In the counterexample, *x* and *y* are physically indiscernible in *W1* because in *W1* they both have the one *P*-property *P'*. Yet in *W1* they do not have the same *N*-properties: In *W1* *x* but not *y* has *N'*. This consequence of D1 seems incompatible with the idea that the nonphysical is determined wholly by the physical.[16]

The nonreductive determinationist might respond that this alleged weakness of D1 is actually a strength. There are plenty of cases in which a nonphysical property of a thing—a biological property, for example—is *not* determined by the thing's *own* physical properties, so that two things that are physically indiscernible can have different biological properties. Recall from Chapter 3 the biological notion of the proper function or purpose of an organ or device or behavior. What the proper function of an organ is, we saw, is a matter of a *history*. To have a given proper function the organ must be a reproduction of an ancestor in a family of organs, which family historically proliferated because a critical mass of the ancestors performed that function.[17]

This means that the organ's present physical structure, constitution, composition, behavior, and indeed all its causal powers are not enough to determine the organ's proper function. If the history is wrong it will not have that function. For example, the proper function of the organ we call the heart is to pump blood. To *be* a heart is to have that function or purpose. Now suppose that by some cosmic accident a collection of molecules hitherto in random motion were to coalesce to form an exact physical duplicate of your heart, the same down to the last microparticle. Because the history of this instant duplicate is wrong—it is not a descendant, not in the family—it would not *be* a heart, even though subsequently, if transplanted quickly enough, it could take over from your heart and perform its function. Generalizing, suppose that by another cosmic accident your exact physical double coalesced next to you. That being would not only have no heart, no liver, no eyes, no brain, it "would have no ideas, no beliefs, no intentions, no aspirations, no fears, no hopes."[18] For all of these depend on certain items' having appropriate proper functions, and again the history would be wrong.

If this account is on the right track, any physicalism or other metaphysics is in trouble if it entails that all the nonphysical properties of a thing are determined solely by something to do with its own structure, constitution, composition, causal powers, or dispositions to behave in certain ways. The alleged difficulty with nonreductive determination is a difficulty for any such metaphysics. It is not a difficulty for D1. D1 is designed with just this kind of case in mind, a case in which whether x possesses some biological or other nonphysical property depends not only on whether x possesses certain physical properties but also on whether other objects, located elsewhere or much earlier in a history, possess various physical properties.

Determination-at-a-Distance

Those who find nonreductive determination problematic might reply that such cases as these do not call for a relation of determination in the sense of D1, even though they are compatible with D1. Such cases can be handled just as well by a generalization account according to which, among other things, for each realized property N that x has there is some complex P of physical properties x has, *including x's relational historical properties*, such that whatever has P has N.[19]

For example, consider an entity that has not only the physical structure and other intrinsic physical properties your heart has but also the same historical relations to ancestor hearts. Any such entity must also have the same biological properties, including the proper function of pumping blood. Because an instant duplicate does not have the same historical relations to ancestor hearts, we are not compelled to say that it has this proper function, or that it is a heart.

Nonreductive determinationists might concede that these kinds of cases by themselves do not favor D1 over a generalization account when the latter is extended to include relational properties. But they do not favor the latter over the former either. We have a standoff, so far as these kinds of cases are concerned. Of course we should tip this balance in favor of a generalization account if the objections to D1 lately canvased are successful and there are no problems for the generalization account. But the reverse is true, and the balance should be tipped the other way—provided the nonreductive determinationist's foregoing replies to these objections are sound.

Furthermore, *there is a closely related kind of case that may spell trouble for a generalization account even when the latter is extended to include relational physical properties.* According to those who urge a generalization account, among the relational physical properties that are to enter into the generalization, some must be *causal.*[20] For each realized nonphysical *N*, there is some complex *P* of physical properties and relations where *P* is to include some causal physical relations, such that whatever has *P* also has *N*. The relation of dependency between a thing's *N*-properties and its *P*-properties is to be one in which its having certain *N*-properties depends on its bearing certain causal physical relations to other things. Given the nonphysical property of having the proper function of pumping blood, there is some complex *P* your heart has such that *P* includes some causal physical relations, and whatever has *P* also has the proper function of pumping blood.

In line with this, let us assume, for the sake of argument, that among the physical relations that are to enter such generalizations, there must be at least one causal one, so that *x* bears this relation to *y* only if there is some *causal* connection between *x* and *y*. Now suppose we were to find a case in which one of x's nonphysical properties N is determined at least in part by something to do with y's physical properties, and yet there is no causal connection between x and y. It would follow that x has no relational physical property that involves bearing some causal physical relation to y. We could not infer there is some complex P that x has such that P includes a causal physical relation between x and y, and whatever has P has N. Instead, whether x has N depends not only on whether x possesses certain physical properties and relations but also on what physical properties y has independently of any causal physical relation to x. This sort of case would be inconsistent with a generalization account even when extended to include causal relational physical properties.

Are there such cases? Consider a creature endowed with beliefs, as are human beings. Whether the creature's beliefs are true can play an important role in our attempts to explain its adaptation or survival in the world. It is because a band of hunter-gatherers acquires true beliefs from returning scouts about conditions over the horizon that the band is more likely to be successful in finding game or forage or shelter. The truth of a belief, according to Millikan's biosemantics, is determined by a world-affair or condition onto which the belief is supposed to map in accordance with a certain mapping rule (as we saw in Chapter 3). It is a consequence of her view, we noted, that in certain cases the affairs mapped may be so distant that no causal chain connects them to the beliefs. Nor need the truth of a particular belief always play a role in explaining survival.

Now suppose I come to believe, perhaps as a result of being kicked in the head, that Saturn's rings contain a certain ammonia molecule.[21] Call it "Ammon." Suppose Ammon is indeed contained in Saturn's rings, so the belief happens to be true (though I have no evidence that it is). Thus one of my belief's nonphysical properties, namely truth, is determined at least in part by something to do with Ammon's physical properties. Yet there is no causal connection between my belief and Ammon. Doubt on this score can be dispelled by changing the example to make Ammon a particle in the rings of a planet outside what physicists call my "backward light cone"; no causal signal, not even light, can reach me from Ammon. Whether my belief is true depends not only on whether it possesses certain physical properties and causal relations, including a physical history, but also on what physical properties Ammon has, even though Ammon's having them cannot result in some causal physical relation between the belief and Ammon. An exact duplicate of my belief, the same even as regards its causal physical relations, could be false, and it would be false if Ammon is not in the rings. Note also that even if there is some relation between Ammon and me which is expressible in the language of physics—a relation that is thus in the broad sense a physical relation—it is not likely to be a relation that does any work in determining that my belief is true, if Millikan's biosemantics is right.[22]

The moral of this example, provided its presuppositions are sound, is at least twofold. First, there are cases that conflict with a generalization account even when extended to include causal physical relations. Second, we should be wary of declaring, prior to adequate empirical investigation, what can depend on what. It may seem completely counterintuitive that our psychological attributes, such as having a particular true belief, are not determined solely by our own physical properties and causal physical relations but can depend on something so trifling and seemingly irrelevant as a single molecule in a distant planet's rings. This seems counterintuitive to those who possess "a strong inclination . . . to look for an explanation of 'global determination' in terms of specific 'local determinations'. . . . Perhaps . . . this is a manifestation of our micro-reductive proclivities."[23]

Those who share such microreductive proclivities are tempted to build exclusions into the determination relation itself, in order to make the relation inconsistent with the dependence of nonphysical attributes on anything so seemingly irrelevant. This provides much of the motivation behind generalization accounts, which tend to build in the exclusions. Because of the exclusions, generalization accounts of determination are often vulnerable to counterexamples that come to light as further empirical observation and theory construction tell us what in the world depends on what. A better policy, according to the nonreductive determinationist (among others), is to explicate determinational dependency without the exclusions, then let empirical inquiry settle the question of what depends on what. But . . .

Global Determination

There is a third moral of the Ammon example. It suggests there may be a counterexample to D1 itself. Suppose that even if there are relations between Ammon and me which are expressible in the language of physics, they are not significant, not relations that do any real work in determining whether my belief is true. Examples of such relations might be "having greater mass than," "being in motion with respect to," "being larger than," "being outside the light cone of," and so on. In this case, there could be two physically possible worlds $W1$ and $W2$ such that in $W1$ my belief x (that Saturn's rings contain Ammon) has exactly the same physical properties *and relations* as my belief y has in $W2$; yet x is true in $W1$ (where Ammon is in the rings) while y is false in $W2$ (where it is not). This would falsify D1.

If physicalists wish to accommodate cases like this, in which a nonphysical property of a thing would not be determined even by the thing's own physical properties *and relations*, they need a better explication of determination. D1 is less exclusionary than generalization accounts, but it too seems influenced by microreductive proclivities that focus on the thing's own physical properties and relations.

What is needed is an explication according to which the physical conditions not only of x but also of things that bear no significant physical relation to x can determine nonphysical matters about x. The needed idea is that two physically possible worlds, the same as regards which physical conditions obtain in them, are also the same as regards which nonphysical conditions obtain in them, even when these are not physical conditions of the same things. For example, suppose two worlds are the same not only as regards the physical conditions of my belief (including its physical relations to other things) but also as regards the physical conditions of the molecules in Saturn's rings and of whatever else may prove relevant. Then the two worlds are also the same as regards whether my belief is true. This suggests the following explication of nonreductive determination:

D2—Given any two physically possible worlds *W1* and *W2*, if the same physical conditions obtain in both, the same nonphysical conditions obtain in both,

where to say that the same physical (or other) conditions obtain in both is to say that for every such condition φ, φ obtains in one if and only if φ obtains in the other. D2 is less a mouthful than D1. Nevertheless it too is sometimes abbreviated by saying that two worlds that are physical duplicates are nonphysical duplicates or that given the way things are physically there is one and only one way they can be nonphysically.

Like D1, D2 entails no connective generalizations, nor does it entail essentialism; the Old Grad counterexamples work here too. Also, D2 is compatible with various relational and historical phenomena that need to be accounted for, including at least one case that may falsify D1 (the Ammon case). There is some irony, then, that D2 was, by several years, the first explication offered for a relation of determinational dependency.[24]

Furthermore, consider the complaint against D2 that it is *too* "global." It says nothing about the *specific* physical conditions *P*, often local, that determine a given nonphysical condition or phenomenon *N*. All D2 says, in effect, is that *somewhere* in the world there are *P*-conditions, possibly scattered, that determine *N*. Surely this is too vague.

But the complaint overlooks an important fact, says the nonreductive physicalist. Once in possession of D2, we can readily explicate the notion of the specific *P*-conditions that determine *N*. Merely define them as the *P*-conditions that form the least set that suffices to determine *N*. To say that they form the least such set is to say that they but no proper subset of them suffice to determine *N*. In this way, D2 enables us to combine specificity with the relational, historical, and holistic thinking involved in much that needs to be accounted for.[25]

This has been a difficult section, as one would expect of life on the frontier. We began by wondering what *positive* account metaphysicians could give of the relation between their unifiers and the rest of the phenomena. If the relation is not reductive, what *is* it? Some physicalist metaphysicians have answered, "Nonreductive determination." Their arguments, provided they hold up, yield an account or explication, in D2, of what the relation is supposed to be. They also clarify how the relation differs from various relations in the neighborhood, why it does not entail either essentialism or reductive generalizations, how it is compatible with the relational and historical phenomena that need to be accounted for, and how it can be used to define the notion of the specific phenomena that do the determining. Even though some physicalists were the first to explore nonreductive determination, other metaphysicians can put it to good use if challenged about the relation between *their* unifiers and the phenomena.

So far, so good (again, provided the nonreductive determinationists' arguments hold up). But it is not enough simply to explicate or define a relation of nonreductive determination and clarify its logical properties. It is not even enough to see how the relation is compatible with various irreducible phenomena that involve the relational or the historical. What we also want is an account of just how the irreducible phenomena arise or emerge from the underlying entities and processes, however distant in space and time. We began the section by wondering about this too. In particular, we wondered just how the intentional properties of an act or thought are supposed to be determined by the way things are at the level of underlying physical entities. "The irony is that the reductive physicalist *does* have an account," if reductivism is right: The reason the intentional properties are determined by the physical properties is that at bottom the intentional properties are really *equivalent* to physical properties, because persons are nothing but physical objects. "It is the nonreductive physicalists . . . who have no account of the properties in question."[26] In the next chapter we consider what reply might be made to this question about intentionality and to related questions about consciousness and value.

NOTES

1. Rorty (1989), 75–81, 96.
2. Feinberg (1966), 5–6.

3. Hellman and Thompson (1975), 552; Hellman and Thompson (1977), 311; Post (1987), sec. 4.0.

4. Churchland (1985), 14, who asserts not only the equivalence of these properties but also their identity.

5. Churchland (1979), (1985); Hooker (1981).

6. Churchland (1985), 26.

7. Campbell (1988), 360–361.

8. Hooker (1987), 282.

9. Kim (1987), 319–320. Kim (1989) extends this and the following arguments.

10. Kim (1987), 321.

11. Petrie (1987), 121, presents this counterexample against a somewhat different entailment-claim. That it also works against the present entailment-claim seems not to have been noticed by Kim (1987), 317, contrary to his argument that McLaughlin's supervenience, which is essentially D1 here, entails strong supervenience, which in turn entails the generalization. In addition it works against his claim that weak supervenience is equivalent to his principle (II).

12. Kim (1987), 320.

13. Kim (1987), 319–322.

14. See also Kincaid (1988).

15. Post (1987), secs. 5.1 and 5.2.

16. According to Kim (1987), 321.

17. Millikan (1984), Chs. 1–2, and Millikan (1989).

18. Millikan (1984), 93.

19. Kim (1987), 323–324.

20. Kim (1987), 323, speaks of *causal*-historical relations and on 322 of *local* determinations. And Kim (1989), 43, says, "mental properties must be *causal properties*."

21. An example derived from Kim (1987), 321, though turned to the opposite effect.

22. See further Ch. 6. This case would also be a counterexample to MND in Post (1987), 176, which says that if *x* and *y* are indiscernible as regards their physical properties and relations, they are indiscernible as regards their nonphysical properties. Thus Margolis (1989), 322, n. 72, is right about MND, though not for the reason he gives. In any case, MND is entailed neither by D1 nor by D2 below; D2 is essentially TT* in Post (1987), 185.

23. Kim (1987), 322.

24. By Hellman and Thompson (1975), 558. D2 is a possible-worlds rendition of their principle (4), though in terms of conditions rather than sentences.

25. Post (1987), 188.

26. Margolis (1989), 220, who concludes that we should declare a plague on both the physicalist houses.

6

METAPHYSICS AND HUMAN BEING

INTENTIONALITY

How can we fit human beings into a scientific or naturalistic metaphysics? We cannot, many philosophers contend, and intentionality is the most basic reason why. A scientific or naturalistic account must be a causal account, they believe, but no causal account can possibly do justice to the intentionality of our thoughts. The intentionality of our thoughts, as of anything else, is a matter of their being directed upon or about something, and this directedness or aboutness cannot be any merely causal affair. For one thing, our thoughts are often about things that do not exist (Santa Claus, unicorns, the ether), and there can be no causal relation to a nonexistent. But even when we are thinking about something that does exist, there may be no causal relation between us and it (as lately seen of Ammon). In either case, the argument continues, that the thought is about something, and what it is about, cannot be determined by our behavior or brain states or anything of the sort. For these will often be causally unaffected by what the thought is about, so that they can be causally the same yet the thought can be about something else or nothing at all. Physical duplicates can be about or represent quite different things.[1]

Furthermore, in order to understand our fellow human beings and to explain why they do certain things, we must often attribute various thoughts to them. Why did Jones go into the garden? Because he thought there was a unicorn there. Why did Columbus sail west?

Because he believed he could reach the East that way. The only remotely adequate explanatory theory of human beings we have is one in which such intentional properties play an essential and irreducible role. Call the theory "folk psychology," if you like, but what could conceivably rival it?

There are rivals, indeed superiors, or so it is claimed. According to *behaviorists*, insofar as it makes sense to ascribe a belief or other intentional state to Jones, Jones's having the belief is simply a matter of how Jones responds, or at least is disposed to respond, to various stimuli or input. The relevant kinds of response can include verbal responses. Suppose Jones is disposed to respond yes when asked whether there is a unicorn in the garden. This disposition is not only *evidence* that Jones believes there is a unicorn in the garden. In addition, the disposition to answer yes and to behave accordingly is just what it *is* to have the belief. So too for the rest of Jones's intentional states. Those who insist that the intentional involves something beyond behavioral dispositions are being unscientific and obscurantist.

Identity theorists, who are not at all unscientific, do hold that the intentional involves something beyond the behavioral. Intentional and other states of the organism, insofar as it makes sense to talk about them, are not to be identified with dispositions to respond in certain ways to sensory input. Rather, they are identical with *physical* states of the organism, including the inner workings, structure, and physical composition of the central nervous system.

Functionalists, who likewise are not unscientific, reject both behaviorism and physical identity theories. Intentional and other states of the organism are to be identified neither with the organism's dispositions to respond in certain ways to sensory input nor with its physical states. Instead, they are to be identified with its *functional* states. A functional state of an organism or machine is first of all an abstract property that can be realized in many ways, much as addition can be performed in many ways by different calculators with their different circuitry, materials, and programs. The same functional state could be realized in many different kinds of "stuff," including nonphysical stuff. Thus functionalists are not necessarily physicalists, though many of them are.

Beyond its abstractness, a functional state is defined by its causal relations not only to sensory input and motor output, as with the behaviorists, but also to other internal states. Thus the causal role of a functional state can be extremely complex. But it need not be very complex to resist definition in purely behaviorist terms. There is a mathematical result to the effect that even a state so simple as to involve only primitive feedback cannot be defined behavioristically.[2] Since most if not all animal nervous systems involve feedback, pure behaviorism would seem not even to be in the running as an account of animal behavior, let alone of something so complex as the human animal.

How do physical identity theories and functionalism fare with beliefs? Let us concentrate on functionalism. For if functionalism fails to account for beliefs, so do identity theories. The reason is that identity theories are narrower than functionalism, since they identify the belief state with a physical state rather than regard the physical state as just one way the belief state might be realized or embodied. According to functionalists, to have a particular belief is just to be in a certain functional state. To believe that there is a unicorn in the garden is for your central nervous system, primarily your brain, to be in or to realize a particular state defined by certain causal relations to sensory input, other brain states, and motor output. To insist that the belief involves more than this is to be, if not unscientific or obscurantist, at least softheaded. How could the existence or the individuation of a psychological state involve something that is not a matter of causal relations to sensory input, other brain states, and motor output?

One reply is that even if having a particular belief requires your brain to be in a certain functional state, it also requires more. The belief, after all, is *directed upon* or *about* something. Functionalism gives no account of this directedness or aboutness. Consider two beliefs, or the two patterns of neuronal activity they are realized in. Suppose they are the same as regards their causal relations to sensory input, other inner states, and motor output. Two such beliefs are thus exactly the same as regards their causal powers. What prevents them from being about quite different things?[3]

Functionalists will tend to regard this sort of question as unintelligible. Two such beliefs *cannot* be about different things. What a belief is about, if the notion is to make any sense, is just a matter of its causal relations to input, other states, and output—nothing more, nothing less. This includes causal relations to distant objects via their causal effects on the organism and its input. Therefore, what a belief is about, what it is "directed upon," is determined without remainder by its causal powers, meaning its causal role. It makes no sense, or at any rate no empirical sense, to imagine two beliefs that are the same as regards their causal powers and yet are about different things.

This is a move in the direction of eliminitivism. Whatever cannot be fitted into the framework, whatever cannot be appropriately reduced, is to be eliminated as the sad remnant of primitive folk psychology. But even though the move is eliminativist, it is not necessarily wrong. Scientific advances often force us to give up cherished heirlooms. Such was the fate of the earth-centered universe, of the brain as an organ for cooling the blood, of the eyes' seeing by sending out beams, of phlogiston, of an earth and its species lately created much as we see them now. Why not also this mysterious directedness or aboutness that allegedly goes beyond the causal powers of a thing?

It will not do simply to reply by appealing to our intuitions. True, many people have strong intuitions to the effect that some thoughts and acts necessarily involve a directedness or aboutness that transcends any causal account. But so too did people have strong intuitions about an earth-centered universe and the origin of species. What we call "intuitions" are nothing more than entrenched ways of conceptualizing things, ways rooted in theories that share the fallibility of all theories.

This applies even to the Ammon example in Chapter 5. Such intuitive obviousness as the example may have could turn out to derive from a misplaced confidence in folk psychology. We may well need a better theory than folk psychology, a better theory of our psychological attributes, including the attribute of having a particular true belief. Such a theory might entail that our psychological attributes must after all be determined solely by matters to which we can be causally related, on pain of the attributes' being judged unreal if they are not so determined. Functionalism claims to be just such a theory. Champions of the reality of irreducible intentionality therefore need a less question-begging reply than appeals to intuition.

One such reply challenges not only functionalism and related theories but also physical identity theories, and challenges them at an elementary level. Minimally, functionalism ought to provide an account of routine functional properties, whether of mechanisms or organisms. But consider again a heart. To *be* a heart is to have the proper function of pumping blood. The biological property of being a heart is evidently a functional property. According to functionalism, this functional property must be a state defined by certain causal relations to input, output, and other states of the thing that is a heart. That is, what makes a thing a heart are its actual causal powers.

According to Millikan, the trouble here is double. First, there are things that have these causal powers but are not hearts. Water pumps are capable of pumping blood, but they are not hearts. Likewise, "Devices have now been designed that in fact pump blood in people, but these are only artificial hearts, not members of the biological category 'heart'."4 Even an instant duplicate of your heart, with therefore precisely the same causal powers, would not be a heart, as we saw in Chapter 5. Second, there are things that are hearts but do not have the causal powers. There are malformed hearts, diseased hearts, injured hearts. Biological functional properties are a matter not of actual causal powers but of a history. No connective generalization holds between the actual causal powers of a thing and its proper function.

Functionalism looks only to the causal powers of things, not to their histories. It must therefore fail as an account of the biological functions not only of hearts but also of lungs, eyes, and brains, if Millikan is right. Now suppose it turns out that the intentionality of a thing—of a certain distribution of neuronal activity, say—is a particular kind of biological function of the thing (where biological function, we recall from Chapter 3, need not be innate, evolved, or wired-in but can be learned, indeed learned very quickly). Then we should expect functionalism and related theories to have a tough time accounting for intentionality without eliminating it. For "intentionality does not reside in a mechanism but in its history."5 Indeed, from Millikan's point of view, functionalism and its kin are on the wrong track entirely.

But *is* intentionality a species of biological function? According to Millikan's theory it is. Anything that has a proper function is *supposed* to do something. Hearts are supposed to pump blood, hoverfly males to catch conspecific females, bee dances to map onto a direction, sentences to map onto configurations of things in the world. Each of these organisms, behaviors, or devices has a purpose, something it is *meant* to do, "which something can be described, yet which something may or may not *be*."[6] But this is the traditional earmark of the intentional. What is intentional is supposed to stand in relation to something else—that which it *intends* or *means* or *is meant to do*—even if that something does not exist or never comes about. Thus "in the broadest possible sense of 'intentionality,' any device with a proper function might be said to display 'intentionality.' "[7]

But in a narrower sense of 'intentionality,' only things like beliefs or sentences have intentionality. Why suppose that *their* intentionality is a matter of their being members of certain biological or proper-function categories? One reason is that we acquired the ability to have beliefs and use sentences by way of a long evolutionary process. The ability to produce and understand sentences with "aboutness" has *survival value*, which is one of the marks of biological proper function. Another and more important reason is that beliefs and sentences can be *defective*, which is a *normative* matter. They can be false, they can fail to be about what they are supposed to be about, and they can fail in other ways. Anything that can be defective displays "the characteristic mark that all things defined by proper-function categories display. . . . What is defective is, just, that which is *not* what it *should* be or can*not* do what it *should* do, hence is something defined by its 'shoulds' rather than by its 'coulds' and 'woulds.' "[8] A third reason, according to Millikan, is that the resulting theory of intentionality has greater explanatory power than its rivals, greater coherence, and a greater capacity to "unravel paradox and produce understanding."

How does the theory work? A review of the section on biosemantics, in Chapter 3, helps us see how a belief or sentence can be a device that exhibits intentionality derived from the proper function of speech-producing and speech-interpreting devices that are a reproduction of an ancestor in a family of devices, which family historically proliferated because a critical mass of the ancestors performed a certain function or functions. In particular, in the case of sentences the derived functions are performed by way of the sentences' mapping onto conditions or world-affairs in conformity to certain rules and thereby having a certain content. The sentences, together with the beliefs they express, thereby exhibit the sort of aboutness or ofness or directedness associated with intentionality. What the sentence is about or represents is the configuration or world-affair onto which it is *supposed* to map in conformity to a certain rule. Biosemantics therefore includes a theory of representation.

Another consequence of biosemantics is that sentences and other devices can exhibit intentionality even if they are neither produced nor interpreted by a conscious being. Indeed, contrary to Brentano and Husserl, "the problem of understanding intentionality can and should be divorced from the problem of understanding consciousness."[9] This means that a naturalist account of intentionality need not also provide an account of consciousness—of pains, of other sensations, of what it is like to fall in love—though of course eventually some account must be given of them as well.

It also means that even though we are often conscious or aware of the intentionality of our thoughts, the awareness affords no guarantee that the thoughts are about something, no guarantee that they are not empty or senseless. For their being about something is in part an external matter, which depends on how other thoughts and the devices that produce them performed in a history over which our present awareness has no say. Indeed, for essentially the same reason, our very *awareness of* something is *itself* partly an external relation, "the inside of the awareness—the feeling part—giving no absolute guarantee that it *is* the inside of a genuine *awareness of* relation." Meaning-rationalism, as we learned to call it in Chapter 3, is therefore false. "Consciousness . . . does not contain *within* it or directly before it an *object* of consciousness. . . . There is nothing diaphanous about consciousness."[10]

Intentionality, then, being a biological proper-function category, is a real phenomenon, every bit as real as other biological categories. The aboutness of a belief is as real as the proper function of the heart, as real as the proper function of a bee dance to map onto a certain direction to nectar. And, like the proper function of the heart or of the dance, neither aboutness in particular nor intentionality in general can be reduced to or identified with the causal powers or physical structure of the devices that exhibit it. One must look to their histories. Moreover, *biosemantics licences the Ammon example*. For biosemantics explains how the truth-conditions of a sentence or belief can include matters not connected to it by any causal chain. According to biosemantics, functionalism and related theories have some explaining to do.

What about philosophies that deny the possibility of *any* naturalistic account of intentionality? Their argument is chiefly that any such account must be a causal account. But Millikan's is a naturalistic account that is not a causal account, in the relevant sense, and it explains why no such account will do. In her view, the mistake of those who deny the possibility of a naturalistic account is to suppose that any such account must be causal. True, they have been abetted in this supposition by those who insist that intentional concepts have no place in science because they have no place in causal explanation. But from Millikan's point of view, this is just the flip side of the same mistake.

What about nonreductive physicalism? What account can *it* give of intentionality? How are the intentional properties of an act or thought supposed to emerge from or be determined by the way things are at the level of the underlying physical entities? These of course are the pointed questions raised at the end of the previous chapter.

Millikan's theory, though naturalistic, is neutral between physicalist and nonphysicalist metaphysics. Nevertheless, nonreductive physicalists, armed with her theory, might reply to the pointed questions as follows. The proper function of a device, as seen, is determined by whether the device is a reproduction of an ancestor in a family of devices, which family historically proliferated because a critical mass of ancestors performed that function (or were correlated with it). But whether one thing is in the intended technical sense a reproduction of another is determined ultimately by whether certain physical causal relations hold between them; so too for whether one thing is an ancestor of another via reproduction.[11] Likewise, whether a critical mass of devices in the reproductive family performed the function is determined ultimately by the physical conditions both of the devices and of their surroundings. Unfavorable physical surroundings "select out" devices that fail to perform. Ill-suited devices fail to be reproduced as often as other devices, which tend to crowd them out.

It follows that proper function is determined ultimately by the physical properties both of the devices, including their ancestor devices, and of their surroundings *in a history*, even though no connective generalization holds between a device's own physical properties and its proper function. So too for the special case of proper function we call intentionality. That an item is about or means or "intends" something, and what it is about or means or "intends," are determined by certain physical properties and surroundings. It is determined not just by the physical properties and surroundings of both the device that produced them and the device's ancestors but also by those of their physical properties and surroundings in virtue of which a critical mass of the ancestors performed a certain function by way of producing items that mapped onto certain configurations. The specific physical phenomena that determine what a belief is about— those that form the least set that suffices to determine this—occur over time, in various places, certainly not all in the head. The nonreductive physicalist is free to deny that beliefs that are physical duplicates must have the same content. In this way physicalists could argue that they can "make room for the requisite concept of content."[12] So too for nonphysicalists: If the things and properties *they* take as the unifiers determine these matters of proper function, they also thereby determine intentionality.

This account relies on the fact that the determination relation is *transitive*. That is, if A determines B, and B determines C, then A determines C. If a metaphysician's unifiers determine matters of proper function, and matters of proper function determine intentionality, then the unifiers determine intentionality. Because determination entails no connective or bridge generalizations or laws, there need be no such generalizations or laws from properties at a lower level to those at a higher (though of course *other* kinds of bridge principles connect them, as in Millikan's theory). There is no need to say—and strong reason to deny—that whatever has certain unifying properties, relations, or causal powers also has a certain proper function.

In particular, there need be no physical explanation of proper function or of intentionality that relies on such generalizations. Nonetheless, the nonreductive physicalist claims that an important kind of explanation or understanding is achieved when we see that and how the physical properties of devices and their surroundings in a history determine matters of proper function and thereby determine intentionality. In this way and in this sense, there is an explanation of how and why the intentional is determined by the physical, even though there is no explanation based on connective generalizations from physical properties to intentional properties.[13] In this sense, it is not "a brute and unexplainable . . . primitive fact about the world" that the one determines the other. Or so the nonreductive physicalist will try to argue, as will nonphysicalist metaphysicians who wish to integrate biosemantics with what they take to be the unifying entities and properties.

CONSCIOUSNESS

"Without consciousness the mind-body problem would be much less interesting. With consciousness it seems hopeless."[14] The mind-body problem is the problem—or a cluster of problems—about what the relation is (or the relations are) between mind and body, the mental and the physical, consciousness and matter.

Different philosophers often use the word 'consciousness' to refer to different things. Here we will use it to refer to what sometimes is called the *subjective* character of experience, sometimes the *qualitative* character. The subjective or qualitative character of an experience includes such things as the immediate, felt character of a painful headache, the sensation of scarlet, how a new car smells inside, what it is like for a person blind from birth suddenly to see. The qualitative character of the experience of scarlet is thought by many philosophers to be that which someone blind from birth cannot grasp or understand about visual experience of the color. In this connection, Locke (1632–1704) tells us that

A studious blind man, who had mightily beat his head about visual objects, and made use of the explication of his books and friends, to understand those names of light and colours which often came in his way, bragged one day, that he now understood what 'scarlet' signified. Upon which, his friend demanding what scarlet was, the blind man answered it was like the sound of a trumpet.[15]

Philosophers today have their own name for the qualitative characteristics or properties of experience—what a person blind from birth supposedly cannot grasp about what it is like to see scarlet. They call them "qualia." The problem, hopeless or not, is that qualia seem to defy *any* kind of objective account, not only physicalist. As a result it is unclear what the relation is between the body and the aspect of mind that qualia constitute, hence between matter and consciousness. Qualia seem to defy integration into what we know of ourselves from science.

Or so it is said. For consider dreams. It is true that what it is like to dream is sometimes hard if not impossible to express, even when we remember the dream; we therefore suspect that someone who never had any dreams could not grasp what it is like. It is also true that, despite this, there is clearly something it is like to dream, something we may call the subjective or qualitative character of dream experiences. There is something distinctive about the qualia of dreams. Any list of what is distinctive about them would include the vividness of the sensory impressions (typically visual) that occur in dreams; the radical discontinuities of time, place, and person (including fantastic violations of physical law); the uncritical acceptance of bizarre events as real; and frequent, powerful emotional involvement. But before concluding that such matters defy scientific accounting, we should see what kind of account is given by contemporary neuroscience.

Among the leading neuroscientific theories or models of dreaming, one finds the recently developed activation-synthesis model (ASM).[16] According to ASM, dreaming occurs when one group of neurons in the brainstem—the "REM-on" group—becomes active, and a certain other group falls silent. The REM-on group sends near-random excitatory impulses to various higher brain centers. (Certain biochemical substances may also be involved—acetylcholine, prostaglandins, cytokines.) In particular, the REM-on group sends impulses to the visual cortex, the motor cortex, and associated cortices and centers of emotion. Input from the external world is simultaneously inhibited. The higher cortex responds to these internally generated signals by sending out motor commands, much as it responds to external signals when we are awake. The motor commands are experienced by the higher cortex, but their execution is blocked in the spinal cord. The dreaming brain then tries to make sense of all these internal and near-random stimuli, including its own responses. It does so by weaving them into a dream-story based on such things as the person's past experiences, present preoccupations, and basic personality:

The brain [is] so inexorably bent upon the quest for meaning that it attributes and even creates meaning when there is little or none to be found in the data it is asked to process. . . . In our dreams we all become writers, painters and film-makers, combining extraordinary sets of characters, actions and locations into strangely coherent experiences.[17]

ASM explains the characteristic qualia of dreams in these terms. The vividness of the dream qualia is due to the preferential stimulation of visual and motor circuits. The bizarre discontinuities reflect the randomness of the impulses from the REM-on cells. Fantastic events are accepted as real because the brain is deprived of the external input it could use to cross-check. Intense feeling arises from the direct stimulation of emotion centers. And the tendency to forget the dream is explained by a correlated lack of stimulation of long-term memory systems.

There is far more to ASM than any thumbnail introduction could possibly convey. But perhaps enough has been said to make us wonder whether the subjective character of dream experience might not have been satisfactorily accounted for by ASM, or at least might be well on the way to being accounted for, either by ASM or by some plausible further development of ASM and related theories. And if the subjective character of dream experience might thus be accounted for, why not also the subjective character of other kinds of experience? Where is the problem, let alone a hopeless one?

One problem, as some philosophers see it, is that even if ASM were known to be entirely true of the brain, indeed even if we knew *all* there is to know about the operations of the brain, this still would not explain the subjective character or the qualia of our experiences. Even total knowledge of the detailed physical operations of the brain must leave something out. Imagine a brilliant neuroscientist, blind from birth, who has mastered all there is to know about the physical structure and activity of the brain, together with the correlations between certain brain states and what normal persons report about their visual experiences. There would still be something the omniscient but blind-from-birth neuroscientist could not explain, and could not even imagine, about the visual experience of those who can see: what it is like to see scarlet, for example, or other colors.[18]

But what makes us so sure that no such explanation could be given? Suppose, though only for the sake of argument, that what it is like to see scarlet is actually *identical* with some brain state. In that case there *would* be an explanation of the subjective character of the experience of seeing scarlet. Total knowledge of the physical operations of the brain and of the correlations between certain brain states and reports of subjective experience would afford an explanation of the subjective character by way of identifying it correctly with a certain brain state. In much the same way do kinetic theories of temperature afford an explanation of temperature by identifying it with mean molecular kinetic energy.

It is true (we may provisionally suppose) that the blind-from-birth neuroscientist could not imagine what it is like to see scarlet. But it would not follow that what it is like is not identical with the brain state. It would follow only that the blind-from-birth neuroscientist could not be in that brain state. To say that nonidentity does follow would be like saying that temperature is not identical with mean molecular kinetic energy, because a physicist deprived from birth of the tactile sense of hot and cold could not imagine what temperature is like, or that the morning star is not identical with the evening star because for some reason some otherwise completely knowledgeable astronomer could not imagine what the evening star is like. Thus the argument from inability-to-imagine does not even show that qualia are not *identical* with brain states, let alone that they are not explainable by them in some weaker sense.[19]

Perhaps what is meant, however, is that even the omniscient neuroscientist could not *deduce* predicates that express what it is like to see scarlet from the physical operations of the brain and would thereby be unable to explain what it is like. But this presupposes that explanation requires such deducibility. Some varieties of explanation do, many do not. Consider the explanation of heat as a certain mean molecular kinetic energy. From just the physical activity of the molecules, one cannot deduce that a roaring hearth will be warm, only that its molecules will have a certain mean molecular kinetic energy. Yet it does not follow that there can be no explanation of heat as a certain mean molecular kinetic energy. It does not even follow that heat is not *identical* with the mean molecular kinetic energy.[20]

The way the explanation works is not by deducing predicates that express warmth and the like from just the physical activity of the molecules. Instead, it works by deducing them from their physical activity *in conjunction with postulated principles that connect warmth with the physical activity*. These connective principles, which are an essential part of kinetic theories of temperature, are what license identifying temperature with mean molecular kinetic energy. In other explanations of other phenomena, the connective principles, which need not and often do not take the form of connective generalizations, may not license nearly so tight a relation as identity. Yet in conjunction with the rest of the principles (chiefly those about the underlying processes—molecular, neural, whatever) they afford an explanation. So even if the neuroscientist cannot deduce predicates that express what it is like to see scarlet from the physical activity of the brain, it does not follow that there is no explanation in terms of this activity conjoined with appropriate connective principles. What we discover in neuroscience is not only the physical activity of the brain but also important explanatory connections and correlations between this activity and our subjective experiences.

But there is another problem for a physicalist account of the subjective phenomena. Suppose we try to express the subjective character of an experience. Sometimes we succeed, often we fail. Occasionally we fail because of insufficient command of our language: There are words to express what it is like to have the experience, but unfortunately they escape us. A skilled novelist or poet, on the other hand, could find the words. At times, though, even a master of the language is doomed to failure; what it is like to have the experience is ineffable. Indeed, some experiences are so alien to those of us who have not had them that, words aside, we cannot even imagine or understand what it is like to have them. But if the subjective character of an experience is not humanly expressible, it is not expressible in neuroscience either. Hence no such expression could appear in the connective principles needed for explanation, and "it is a mystery how the true character of [the] experiences could be revealed in the physical operation of [the] organism."[21]

Actually the problem is more general than this would suggest. "Conscious experience . . . occurs at many levels of animal life."[22] Given any species with some minimum level of neural complexity, there is something it is like to be a member of that species. In Nagel's striking example, there is surely something it is like to be a bat. But because of the bat's peculiar physiology—especially its sonar—the bat's experience is bound to be fundamentally alien to ours. Hence "we cannot form more than a schematic conception of what it *is* like."[23] What it is really like to be a bat is "beyond the reach of human concepts." This means there are facts—facts about what it is like— "that do not consist in the truth of propositions expressible in a human language."[24] The peculiarity of these facts is that they "are accessible only from one point of view"—that of the subject. If we try to express them in language that abstracts away from point of view, as does the objective idiom of the sciences, we are sure to fail.

Even when some experience does prove expressible in human language, it remains inexpressible in the language of science. It follows that "if we acknowledge that a physical theory of mind must account for the subjective character of experience, we must admit that no presently available conception gives us a clue how this could be done."[25]

What then of ASM, the physical theory of dreaming sketched above? Suppose ASM were presented as a reductive account, according to which (among other things) the subjective characteristics of dreams—their qualia—are either to be identified with or in some other way reduced to purely physical properties of the organism or else to its functional states. The piercing vividness of a dream, its haunting emotional impact, would be equivalent either to some physical pattern of neuronal activity or to a functional state realized in some such pattern.

This kind of reducibility would entail expressibility in objective terms. For suppose that a property N is reducible to, and therefore is equivalent to, a property P. This means that, necessarily, an item x has N if and only if it has P. Suppose further that P is expressible in given terms T (physical, say, or functional), meaning that there is such a term T for which, necessarily, T is true of x if and only if x has P. It follows that, necessarily, x has N if and only if the term T is true of x, which is to say that N is expressible in T-terms too.

But this expressibility in objective terms is just what Nagel's argument, if sound, shows is impossible. The heart of his argument is an "objection to the reducibility of experience. . . . The reduction can succeed only if the species-specific viewpoint is omitted from what is to be reduced."[26] In this process of reduction or translation, the subjective character of the experience will be left out. For objectification omits the subjective point of view precisely because viewing things objectively is to view them, so far as possible, from no particular point of view. And if the subjective character is omitted, it is not expressed by any physical or other objective term T, from which it follows that there is no expressible physical property equivalent to the nonphysical character in question. Therefore, reducibility fails, and the subjective character of experience cannot be accounted for by physicalism, functionalism, or any other objective approach.

But what if ASM is *not* presented as a reductive account? Then Nagel's and other antireductive arguments would lose their grip. The physical theorist of mind need not claim that what it is like to be the subject is reducible to objective terms, hence expressible by them. Instead, the claim would be that what it is like is *non*reductively determined by such physical matters as brain chemistry and which groups of neurons fire in which sequence. And in fact ASM does *not* say that the vividness of a dream is *identical with* or *reducible to* or *nothing but* preferential activation of visual circuits by the acetylcholine-stimulated, REM-on group of neurons. Rather, ASM appears committed only to certain *correlations* between the characteristic qualia of dreams and various patterns of neuronal discharge.

For example, brains and qualia are so correlated that whenever your brain is like mine as regards whether or not the REM-on group is active, you and I are alike as regards whether we are dreaming. Generalizing, whenever our brains are alike in relevant neuronal respects, we are alike as regards the vividness and other subjective characteristics of our dreams, whether or not we can express them.[27] But this is just the *determination* correlation. Thus ASM can be construed as asserting only that the neuronal activity determines what it is like to dream. What ASM says, or tends to say, is that the characteristic qualia of dreams are "the natural concomitant of," "due to," "produced by," "arise or result from," "reflect," or are "associated with" certain neuronal activity. This is to say in effect that the former is determined by the latter. ASM is a connective theory, backed by observed correlations, which provides ample evidence that the subjective character of dreams is determined by what goes on in the brain. Or so nonreductive physicalists may try to argue.

Armed with neuroscientific theories like ASM, physicalists will try to argue further that all subjective phenomena whatever, not only dreams, are nonreductively determined by physical phenomena. If and to the extent that the subjective character of some experiences is influenced by their *intentionality*, as many philosophers believe, physicalists may be expected to appeal to their nonreductive account of the extracranial matters involved in intentionality. In their view, the physical phenomena determine the subjective phenomena in the four-fold sense of determining (a) that there are such phenomena, (b) which ones there are, (c) what they are like, and (d) any other features they may have. Because determination does not entail reducibility, expressibility is beside the point. Physicalists need not "insist that everything real must be brought under an objective description,"[28] nor need other, nonphysicalist metaphysicians do so who wish to account for the subjective phenomena by starting from objectively existing unifiers.

An objective starting point, it might be thought, accords priority to the objective and relegates the subjective to subordinate status. All this talk of how the subjective phenomena are determined by objective affairs smacks of metaphysical imperialism. But while it is true that much traditional metaphysics is imperialistic, we have seen repeatedly that it need not be and that such priority as a metaphysician might claim for objectively existing unifiers is highly conditional. *If*, in a given context, we are interested in what exists independently of consciousness and conceptual scheme and in what its activity might determine about the rest of what there is, *then* objective existence enjoys a certain priority. But the priority will always be conditional upon this interest. In other contexts, the subjective often takes priority, as for example when we need to understand what it is like to be this exciting person we've just met or, more generally, what it is like to be human.

Since there are so many contexts in which we may find ourselves and so many kinds of interest we may take in the world and in each other, we may well wonder which context we ought to be in, on a given occasion, and what kind of interest we should be taking in things. When should we pursue something like the Thales project, and when should we learn from poets, novelists, and historians what it is like to be human in a certain place and time? When should we try unifying the phenomena by reference to objectively existing things, and when should we unify them by a map in polar coordinates centered on us? And what kind of "should" is this, or what kinds? Is there a fact of the matter as regards the value judgments involved in deciding what I should do? Are there objective values?

VALUE

Antirealism and Meaninglessness

"There are no objective values."[29] So goes the majority opinion among philosophers in the twentieth century. The claim is not only that there are no extra *entities* called values—no transcendent objects beyond the ordinary furniture of the world, perhaps beyond space and time—that somehow inject value and meaning into the world. There are not even any normative *properties* things can objectively have or fail to have independently of our subjective responses to them. There is no objective truth of the matter about whether a sunset is beautiful, a killing is evil, or a way of life is good. A complete account of the world does not include any such truths or properties; to be is to be value-neutral or inert, so far as having any objective value is concerned.

This antirealism about value can seem to threaten the very meaningfulness of our lives. If our most cherished ideals have no value grounded in reality, if they therefore have no value independent of our transient desires to achieve them, it seems they cannot be objectively worthwhile. But according to many, only the conviction that our ideals are objectively worthwhile can summon us to live, suffer, fight, and die for them. Destroy the conviction and you destroy the very meaningfulness of our lives.

Most antirealists among Anglo-American philosophers reject this conclusion. Antirealism about value, they argue, entails no such meaninglessness. Ideals can be worth dying for even if they are not objectively grounded in reality. "To realize the relative validity of one's convictions and yet stand for them unflinchingly, is what distinguishes a civilized man from a barbarian."[30] The belief that one's ideals are worthwhile—even the belief that they deserve defending to the death—can be justified without supposing they are grounded in or determined by reality.

One way to justify ideals or to try, at least for moral values, is to update Kant's argument that morality is grounded in the nature of reason. "The ground of obligation . . . must not be sought in the nature of man or in the circumstances in which he is placed, but sought *a priori* in the concepts of pure reason."[31] Immoral acts are acts contrary to reason; they are irrational acts. For they are inconsistent with one of the basic presuppositions of rationality. This is the *categorical imperative*, according to which I must always act in line with a rule or maxim that can without logical absurdity be made a universal law governing *everyone's* actions. If the consequences of *everyone's* acting in accord with the rule would be absurd, *no one* should, myself included. For example, suppose everyone were to follow the rule, Tell a lie. This would be self-defeating, hence absurd; lying would soon become impossible because no one would ever be believed; therefore, no one should lie. Kant hoped to show in this way that morality is more than just a matter of our transient desires and interests, even if it is not grounded in reality in the sense of being true about how things are in reality.

There is another way one might try to justify the belief that a certain act or policy is worthwhile. According to the "ideal observer theory," an act or policy is right if it would be approved by a fully informed, completely impartial and sympathetic observer or spectator. Not that there need actually *be* such an ideal observer. The point rather is to imagine there is one, then ask what it would approve. According to a number of antirealists, what an ideal observer would approve would mostly coincide with traditional morality. In this view, therefore, antirealism about value does not undermine morality. As for the rest of our values—esthetic, social, religious, whatever—the ideal observer theory might be generalized to cover them; a sunset is truly beautiful if the ideal observer would find it so. If some such theory works, antirealism does not entail that life is meaningless or absurd.

Some antirealists, however, far from rejecting the conclusion that life is meaningless or absurd, actually embrace it. They tend to be European philosophers in the existentialist tradition. Because there are no objective values, they argue, responsibility for the choices we make cannot be avoided by pretending they are forced on us by independent values. That way lies "bad faith," an extreme instance of which would be the plea that "the Devil made me do it." Instead, we must make our own choices, from moment to moment, taking full responsibility for them. Since there are no objective values or external duties, what we decided yesterday need not carry over to today. We must either reaffirm the choice or decide differently. Failure to recognize that life is absurd is itself a form of bad faith.

Antirealism about value may or may not entail that life is absurd. But it does entail atheism. The theist believes that God is the source or ground of certain kinds of value, including perhaps above all *moral* value. In creating the world, God brought it about that certain actions and policies are morally right and others morally wrong and that their rightness and wrongness are not based on our wishes, desires, or self-interest. Objective moral values are grounded in reality by being grounded ultimately in God; they are not grounded in human reason or in some fictional ideal observer. It follows that if there are no objective values, there is no God either; antirealism about values entails atheism. Conversely, if there is good reason to believe in God, there is good reason to believe in at least some objective values, the moral values in particular. Theism entails realism about at least the moral values.

Realism, however, does not entail theism. A number of contemporary moral realists, for example, are cheerfully atheist. They believe that there is an objective truth of the matter in morals and that what determines such truth is not God or any other divinity. What determines moral truth are ordinary, naturally occurring properties of things and people. Furthermore, the moral values these realists think are thus determined to be the objectively correct ones tend to coincide with traditional Judeo-Christian-Islamic morality at its best.

The Arguments from Disagreement and Queerness
Is there some way to settle the dispute between moral realists and antirealists? Moral realists emphasize a number of difficulties with antirealism. One difficulty is that our ordinary language and argument about moral issues presuppose there is a truth of the matter.

Most of us believe that discharging toxic waste into someone's drinking water is morally intolerable. When we argue with representatives of industry and government that the practice ought to be stopped—in our neighborhood, right now—the issue is not whether there is a truth of the matter about the immorality. Even the representatives dispatched to placate outraged citizens would agree not only that there is a truth of the matter but also that such discharge, were it occurring, would indeed be immoral. Instead, the debate typically rages over how toxic the waste really is, how much is actually being discharged, whether the chemicals in the water have some other source, what it would cost to clean up, how many jobs would be lost if the company moved, and so on.

Furthermore, on those occasions when a moral belief *is* challenged—say, the belief that abortion is morally permissible during the first trimester—typically we try to defend the belief, however haltingly, by arguing from various facts of the case and from general principles themselves deemed true. Our normal practice of giving reasons for and against moral beliefs is a practice that treats them like beliefs that are true or false. Our ordinary language and argument about morals seem mostly to be realist in character. Nor is this very surprising, given that much of the language has historical roots deep in the theism present at the creation of much of our culture.

Antirealists respond by conceding that our ordinary language and argument about moral matters do presuppose some form of realism. But presuppositions can prove wrong, no matter how widespread and deeply entrenched. So it is with this one. Our ordinary thought and reasoning about morals are massively in error. There really are no objective values.

Anyone who advances this or any other "massive-error thesis" shoulders the burden of proof to show that it is right. For the error, if it is one, is massive precisely because so much of the evidence—or what we take to be evidence—has seemed for so long to so many intelligent people to go the other way. To deny that all this apparent evidence really is evidence is definitely to swim upstream.

Some antirealists try to discharge the burden of proof by means of the "argument from disagreement" (AD) against objective values (sometimes called the "argument from relativity"). Were there objective values, says AD, as there are objective facts in science, presumably they would provide some guide for our beliefs about them, much as observation of things guides hypotheses in science. We could expect that our beliefs eventually would converge on the moral truth of the matter or at least show improvement over earlier beliefs, as happens in science. But when we look at the long, confused history of moral dispute, we see no such thing. What we see are interminable quarrels between parties whose positions are relative to their self-interest, their desires, their moral preconceptions and biases, their culture. Nor do we see any prospect of a method for achieving agreement among them. So too for other values. Therefore, AD concludes, there are no objective values.

Realists reply that AD greatly exaggerates the amount of agreement in science, just as it exaggerates the amount of disagreement about values. Some realists claim further that history does reveal improvement in beliefs at least about moral values; where slavery once was tolerated, for example, now it is universally condemned. But the most serious flaw in AD, they claim, is that it assumes there is only one good explanation of the amount of disagreement about value. The explanation is supposed to be that there are no objective values which would attract agreement or around which agreement could coalesce.

There is a better explanation, says the realist. There are objective values, all right, but often the truth of the matter about them is extraordinarily complex. Science, by comparison, especially natural science, has it easy. Furthermore, people frequently have powerful, self-interested motives for insisting that their position is the morally correct one—motives so strong as to compel them on occasion to deny even plain truth. Neither chemical company employees with families to feed nor parents distraught over their children's drinking water are likely to be cool paragons of dispassionate objectivity. Little wonder, then, in light of the complexity of many moral issues and the partisan passions involved, that their history is one of widespread and continuing disagreement.

A number of antirealists concede that AD, by itself, does not show there are no objective values about which to disagree. AD needs to be backed by an argument that explains why, even though disagreement in science does not imply there really is no truth of the matter about which to disagree, disagreement about values does. The leading candidate for this further and deeper argument is the "argument from queerness" (AQ).[32]

According to AQ, objective values would have to be very queer sorts of things. The reason is that their relation to what clearly is the case or to what everyone admits there is would be highly mysterious. The alleged values are not logically *derivable* from or entailed by the nonnormative or natural properties of things, as Hume taught us long ago. In slogan form, the point is that *ought* cannot be derived from *is*. Even Sartre, who hails from a later and very different tradition, urges the same point: "Ontology . . . cannot formulate ethical precepts. It is concerned solely with what is, and we cannot possibly derive imperatives from ontology's indicatives."[33] Nor can the values be *reduced* to natural properties, as G. E. Moore (1873–1958) taught us. Consider some such proposed reductive equivalence, say between moral goodness and being conducive to the greatest happiness of the greatest number. These two properties seem not to be equivalent. For we can easily imagine someone who both sees that *x* is conducive to the greatest happiness of the greatest number and yet wonders whether *x* is morally good. This shows that it is an open question whether *x* is morally good (hence the name "open-question argument" for this argument against reducibility).

AQ concludes that the alleged objective values or qualities are related to natural properties neither by derivation nor by reduction. Since no other relation has been spelled out that does the job, the alleged objective values must be very queer things indeed. "How much simpler and more comprehensible the situation would be if we could replace the moral quality with some sort of subjective response which could be causally related to the detection of the natural features on which the supposed quality is said to be consequential."[34] What we call objective values are just our subjective attitudes projected onto the value-neutral real world.

In one form or another, AQ is what makes antirealists suspect that our normal moral usage and argument are massively in error. And it is AQ, suitably elaborated, that drives them, despite all difficulties, to maintain that there are no objective values. AQ articulates their feeling that no one has explained how an objective ethics is *possible*. And "it is because we do not see how an objective ethics is *possible* that we worry about irresolvable moral disagreements."[35] If it is to be possible, there must be some unmysterious, unqueer relation between the alleged objective values and natural features of people and things in the world. But what *is* this relation? Evidently it is neither derivation nor reduction. Yet the only plausible alternative is a *causal* relation between stimulation by natural features and our subjective responses to such stimulation. Therefore there are no objective values, and the long history of irresolvable disagreement about value is explained. What really exist are, primarily, the value-neutral, natural, objective features of things and, secondarily, our subjective attitudes toward those features or their effects on us.

Queerness and Proper Function

One reply to all this is that AQ proves too much. Were it sound, it would show not only that there can be no objective values but also that there can be no proper functions. Since hearts, for example, are defined by their proper function of pumping blood, there could be no hearts. That AQ does have this absurd consequence may be seen as follows. The proper function of a device is not derivable from or reducible to any combination of its natural features, including its causal powers. Even an instant duplicate of your heart, with exactly the same natural features, would not be a heart (as we saw in Chapter 5). So the relation between the proper function of a thing and its natural features is not one of derivation or reduction. Therefore, proper functions must be very queer affairs indeed. Their relation to the natural features of the things that have them is quite mysterious, being a relation neither of derivation nor of reduction. How much simpler and more comprehensible the situation would be if we replaced the proper function with some sort of subjective response that could be causally related to our detection of the natural features on which the supposed function is said to be consequential. Objectively speaking, there are no proper functions. What we call proper functions are nothing but projections of our subjective classification schemes onto what clearly and unqueerly *is* there.

Defenders of AQ might reply that this only shows we have not looked widely enough for the relevant natural features. We need to look also at the natural features of the *ancestor* devices and their surroundings in a history. Proper functions are either derivable from or reducible to these further natural features. They are not so queer after all.

The problem with this reply is that even though proper functions are determined by, and in that sense explainable by, these natural features of things and their surroundings in a history, it does not follow that proper functions are either derivable from or reducible to them. For as we've seen, such determination and explanation can obtain in the absence of any connective generalizations from one to the other. Nor does Millikan's theory seem compatible with any such generalizations from the natural features of things in a history to some given thing's proper function. Yet such generalizations are required for reduction and derivation.

To some philosophers it will come as no surprise that AQ threatens to eliminate proper functions. For in many ways AQ reflects and recapitulates a tradition of thought that began in the seventeenth century with the rise of modern science. The rise of the new physics in particular led many to think that what really or primarily exist are the kinds of things physics talks about: extension, solidity, mass, force, impact. The only kind of causation here is "efficient causation" via impact and other direct action of one thing on another ("no action-at-a-distance"). Other matters were thought to be mere appearance or at least to have only derivative or secondary existence. This gave rise to the distinction between the primary and the secondary qualities of a thing (the former including its extension, mass, and the like; the latter its taste, smell, color, and sound). Since the language of physics contains no value judgments, values seemed to form no part of the real world; they are queer sorts of things.

Furthermore, the language of physics contains no terms for the purpose or goal or end of a thing. The contrast with medieval Aristotelian science could not be greater. Many an Aristotelian explanation of events was in terms of a thing's proper end or place, its *telos*. The reason an unsupported object falls, went one such account, is that it seeks its proper place or element, the earth. This is an appeal to the event's "final cause." But early modern science ridiculed all such teleological explanations, all final causes, and with them all talk of the purpose, end, or proper place or function of a natural object. Indeed, to this day teleological notions are widely suspect because they appear not to be derivable from or reducible to efficient causal relations among natural objects; they are not sufficiently "mechanistic." This amounts to a kind of argument from queerness against teleological notions in general, of which the notion of proper function is a special case. It is partly because of these lingering suspicions that Millikan devotes two rather technical chapters to defining precisely what proper functions are, how they emerge in a history, and how they figure solidly in respectable biological and other scientific explanations.[36]

Millikan's account of how proper function is determined by natural features in a history might suggest a way out of these troubles. Defenders of AQ might agree that proper function is not derivable from or reducible to the relevant natural features in a history. But it *is* nonreductively *determined* by them. Thus a slight amendment to AQ is all that is needed. The argument should be amended to read that since objective values are not derivable from, reducible to, or *determined by* the natural features, their relation to what there admittedly is is so mysterious that we ought to conclude there are none. Call this argument "broadened AQ." Broadened AQ is to allow proper functions but excludes objective values.

The problem here is that just as AQ is *too narrow*, in that it excludes proper function, broadened AQ is *too broad*. For it allows an important class of objective values and therefore cannot be used to show there are no objective values whatever. The reason is simple. Broadened AQ allows proper functions. But the proper function of a thing is what it is *supposed* to do, what it *should* or *ought* to do. Proper function is something defined by a thing's "shoulds" or "oughts" rather than its "does-es" or "coulds" or "woulds." The notion of a proper function is emphatically a normative one. The proper function of a thing is what it *should* or *ought* to do, its *purpose* or biological *value*, regardless of what it in fact does or could or would do. The purpose, function, or biological value of a heart is to pump blood. The purpose, function, or biological value of sperm is to fertilize ova. The purpose, function, or biological value of bee dances, sentences, and beliefs is to map onto affairs in the world. Call these values *proper-function* values. There is nothing mysterious or queer as regards realism about proper-function values.

Antirealists are likely to reply by conceding that indeed there are or may well be objective proper-function values. But it is unfair to make such a fuss over them. What antirealists have really been concerned to reject, after all, are objective values of certain *other* kinds. They have been concerned to reject objective *moral* values in particular but also esthetic, social, and religious values, among others. Even though broadened AQ allows objective proper-function values, it excludes these. For no one has shown how moral values, for example, could be determined by the natural features of things.

But is it so clear, counters the realist, that moral values are not determined by natural features? After all, it is only recently that philosophers have thought to apply a relation of nonreductive determination (or supervenience) to moral values. It seems premature to conclude that moral values cannot be nonreductively determined by the relevant natural features. This contrasts with a much longer history of careful discussion of derivation and reduction between ought and is. This longer history persuades many philosophers that ought cannot be derived from or reduced to is. There is as yet no comparable body of research on the question of nonreductive determination of ought by is.

Bioethics
Furthermore, recall how intentionality, according to Millikan's theory, turned out to be a species of or determined by biological proper function. How can we be so sure that morality, or crucial parts of it, will not also turn out to be a species of or determined by proper function? If it does, then just as natural features of ancestor devices and behaviors and their surroundings in a history determine intentionality, so too for morality.

A big if? Perhaps not. The same considerations that made it

plausible to think of intentionality as a proper-function category seem also to apply in the case of morality. Anything that has a proper function is *supposed* to do or be something, "which something can be described, yet which something may or may not *be*." So too for certain behaviors or acts, which are supposed to be as described by some moral norm or rule, yet may not be. And of course the behaviors and devices to which moral judgments apply can be defective. They can be immoral, impermissible, evil, or irresponsible. Anything that can be defective displays the characteristic mark that all things defined by proper-function categories display.

Furthermore, many philosophers believe that morality has survival value, which is another mark of biological proper function. Hobbes (1588–1679) believed that morality basically coincides with long-term self-interest (that is, with rational egoism). The norms or rules farsighted, rational persons who are concerned with their own survival and flourishing would follow are essentially the rules of traditional morality. Some contemporary philosophers revise and elaborate this Hobbesian approach to argue further, "While it is normally prudent to be moral, it is sometimes rational to be moral even if it is not prudent."[37]

Despite the tie between morality and long-term rational self-interest, Hobbes thought that only through the coercive power of a strong central authority could people and states be made to cooperate in accord with altruistic norms or rules. Such cooperation could not emerge naturally or spontaneously, since each would fear that the other might take advantage of any lapse from vigilant defense of immediate self-interest. But recently some biologists, philosophers, and political scientists have argued in detail that certain altruistic, cooperative behaviors or strategies, by contrast with purely selfish, noncooperative ones, bestow a selective advantage on both the species and the individuals who adopt them. Such strategies are viable, robust, and stable: viable, in that they can gain a foothold even in predominantly noncooperative environments; robust, in that they can thrive in a variety of environments in which others use different strategies; and stable, in that once established they resist invasion by alien strategies. Thus these cooperative strategies will emerge spontaneously in a wide variety of circumstances. So too for cooperation among individuals and states in various institutional and other contexts.[38] "Under suitable circumstances, cooperation can develop even between antagonists," as it did in "the live-and-let-live system that emerged in the bitter trench warfare of World War I."[39]

In view of all this, we might plausibly speculate that a certain kind of behavior or act exhibits morality—that is, has various moral properties—by virtue of being a reproduction of an ancestor in a family of behaviors or acts, which family historically proliferated because a critical mass of the ancestors performed a particular function or functions by conforming to a certain strategy or norm or rule. In short, *the natural features of things and their surroundings in a history determine the moral properties of this kind of act or behavior.* Just what the relevant functions and strategies or rules are would have to be spelled out in any adequate connective theory of morality developed along these lines. Here it is enough to note that the possibility of some such connective theory means that the argument from queerness, even in its broadened form, hardly proves there is no fact of the matter about moral values. And there are other theories, not biological in inspiration, that nonreductively connect morality to various natural features in such a way as to imply determination of the former by the latter. Or so realists will argue.

Realists will argue further that unless and until some other queerness argument can be constructed to show how objective moral values are impossible in principle, antirealists have failed to discharge their burden of proof for their massive-error thesis. The thesis, again, is that our ordinary moral language and argument, entrenched for millenia, are massively in error in presupposing that moral beliefs are true or false. The argument from disagreement is powerless by itself to support a thesis of massive error. AD needs the backing of AQ or at least of broadened AQ.

An Argument for the Determinacy of Valuation

Since the massive-error thesis has not been proved even with the help of broadened AQ, according to the realist, the weight of the evidence from our ordinary language and argument favors the presupposition that moral beliefs are true or false. The presupposition is further supported by the bioethics sketched above, according to which the truth or falsity of a moral judgment is determined by the natural features of things and their surroundings in a history. At the very least, we are entitled to assume a general principle called "metaethical antirelativism" (MEA):

MEA—Two genuinely conflicting moral beliefs cannot both be correct; one only is correct, even if we have no idea which one it is.

Metaethical *relativists*, on the other hand, believe that two genuinely conflicting moral judgments *can* both be correct; there is nothing like a truth of the matter here, so that whatever "correctness" comes to it does not behave like truth. If you judge that euthanasia is never permissible while someone else insists it is sometimes the right thing to do, these two judgments genuinely conflict yet can both be correct. MEA denies this: Just one is correct, even if we do not know which one.

Even though moral realists are committed to MEA, so are a number of people who are not realists. For MEA does not entail realism. One reason is that the "correctness" MEA talks of need not amount to truth, let alone truth in some realist sense of correspondence. Correctness might instead be a matter of the sum total of our evidence to date. Another reason is that even if moral correctness amounted to realist truth, the correctness might not be determined by natural features of people and things in the world. Indeed, so far as MEA goes, moral correctness need not be determined by anything further at all.

Since MEA does not entail realism, MEA can be assumed in various arguments without begging the question against antirealists. In particular, MEA can figure as one of the premises in a deductive argument for the conclusion that moral correctness *is* determined by natural features of people and things in the world. What would such an argument look like? The needed argument requires another premise.[40] In slogan form, this additional premise is that we are to treat like cases alike. For example, if St. Francis is morally good, so is anyone who is like St. Francis as regards natural properties or features. There can be no moral difference without some natural difference. This amounts to what may be called the "equity principle" (EP):

EP—Two items alike as regards their natural features must also be alike as regards their moral status (good, bad, permissible, impermissible, obligatory, and so on).

EP is widely thought to be unproblematic and is accepted by both realists and antirealists.

Given these two premises, EP and MEA, the argument for the determinacy of moral valuation goes as follows. Consider two physically possible worlds $W1$ and $W2$ that are the same as regards the natural features of the people and things in them (natural relations and histories included). In light of EP, it follows that $W1$ and $W2$ are also the same as regards the moral status of the people and things in them. A judgment about moral status is correct in $W1$ if and only if it is correct in $W2$. Furthermore, in light of MEA, this correctness is not relative to the moral beliefs or principles one happens to hold. Instead, a moral judgment is correct or not in $W1$ and $W2$, independently of one's own moral beliefs, so that in a set of conflicting judgments one only is correct, even if we have no idea which one it is.

It follows that for any two physically possible worlds, if the people and things in them are the same as regards their natural features, the same moral judgments are correct in them. But by definition D2 of determination (Chapter 5), this is just to say that moral correctness is determined by natural features of people and things in the world. Given the way the world is as regards the natural features, there is one and only one way it can be as regards which moral judgments are correct. In this sense the correctness is not *made* by us but *found*.

Realists will add that since moral correctness is determined by the natural features, there is a fact of the matter as regards such correctness, and we might as well call our moral judgments true or false. Furthermore, a plausible generalization of this argument for determinacy covers nonmoral values as well (esthetic, social, religious, and so on). Simply generalize EP and MEA so that they are about these other kinds of values too.

Antirealists will reply by rejecting one of the premises of the argument for determinacy. Since EP is harmless, MEA must go. But the standard way of moving against MEA is now blocked. The standard move is first to argue, via AD, that the history of interminable moral disagreement is best explained by there being no objective correctness; the only plausible sort of correctness here is one in which genuinely conflicting moral judgments can all be correct. Yet as we have seen, AD supports this metaethical relativism only if AD is backed by some sort of queerness argument. When we analyze queerness arguments against the very possibility of objective values, even broadened AQ appears unpersuasive. It neglects a number of theories that connect morality to various natural features in such a way as to imply nonreductive determination of the former by the latter. Perhaps none of these theories ultimately works, but purveyors of queerness arguments have not been successful in taking us step by step through each such theory in order to explain just where it is supposed to fail. Or so realists have argued.

Realists about valuational properties may go on to emphasize, as we saw realists emphasize in Chapter 2, that realism does not entail that there is such a thing as *the* way the world is, or just one true and complete characterization of the world, even in terms of value. Likewise, there need be no totalizing unification of everything in terms of some one kind of property, valuational properties included. Nor need there be any appeal to a transcendental or noumenal reality, beneath or beyond the natural features of the world, as that which makes our true value judgments true. The natural features will do quite well, granting the argument for the determinacy of valuation.

Furthermore, nothing in the realist position entails that principles of morality, for example, or principles about other kinds of value are unchanging or the same, regardless of the historical circumstances of those to whom they apply. What the correct principles are is determined by the natural features of people and things; if the latter change in fundamental ways, the former may change too; circumstances alter cases. To say that there is a truth of the matter in morals (or in anything else) and that this truth is determined by how things are objectively in the world is *not* to say or imply there is one true principle that applies always and everywhere. The realist can agree: "Principles are not the less sacred because their duration cannot be guaranteed."[41] Indeed, at a recent conference on moral realism, one heard the quip, "Moral realism does not mean your parents were always right."

Tradition has it that physicalists must be subjectivists or antirealists about value. After all, it was Democritus himself who taught that because there are only atoms and the void, our values are mere conventions. This Democritean inference to "mere conventions" presupposes that values are not determined by the physical phenomena or by what there really is. Today's Democriteans also presuppose this and believe it is proved by the failure of all efforts to establish determination by way of derivation or reduction. But if the physical phenomena nonreductively determine the natural features of things, as physicalists contend, and if the natural features in turn likewise determine value, as the argument for the determinacy of valuation claims, then the physical phenomena determine value after all.

All metaphysicians, not just physicalists, may take advantage of this transitivity of determination. If *their* unifiers suffice to determine the natural features of things, then automatically the unifiers suffice to determine value too, granted the determinacy of valuation. In some such way can theorists of being *qua* being ground objective values in what there is, thereby achieving an ideal of many philosophers from Plato on. Yet ontologists can also agree with Sartre when he says, "Ontology . . . cannot formulate ethical precepts. It is concerned solely with what is, and we cannot possibly derive imperatives from ontology's indicatives." The reason one can follow both Plato and Sartre is that the imperatives can be grounded in what there is, in the sense of being determined by what there is, even if such grounding by itself, being nonreductive, enables no one to derive the imperatives from ontology's indicatives.

Indeed, it is no longer so clear that ontology, or metaphysics, can or should speak only in indicatives. For if the values are determined by what there is, the normative properties of people and things are certainly among the ways they are, and the metaphysician would be remiss in speaking of them only in the indicative rather than in the rich tapestry of other moods needed to express the diverse values and meanings of all the things in our world. A theory of being *qua* being would be remiss if it gave the impression that to be is to be value-neutral, inert, or dead. From this point of view, metaphysics is as much a matter of values as of what there is.

What about the value or meaning of the metaphysician's own unifiers? There are occasions on which we ought not be preoccupied with anything like the Thales project. On such occasions, the unifiers do not take priority but are much less significant than, say, what it is like to be human at this time and place. Suppose the values, including the "oughts," are determined by, and in that sense are a manifestation of, the unifiers. Then it follows that one of the ways in which the metaphysician's unifiers manifest themselves is in their own occasional insignificance and in the occasionally far greater significance of other things, including what it is like to be us, experiencing time and death as we do, and love and mystery and more.

NOTES

1. Baker (1987), 167, who, however, does not reject a naturalistic account, only a physicalistic one.
2. Nelson (1969), 445–446.
3. Baker (1987), 51–59, presses this question and argues that it is fatal for functionalism.
4. Millikan (1984), 17.
5. Millikan (1984), 339, n. 3.
6. Millikan (1984), 95.
7. Millikan (1984), 95. See also Millikan (1986).
8. Millikan (1984), 94.
9. Millikan (1984), 12.
10. Millikan (1984), 91–92.
11. Millikan (1984), 19–23, 27–28.
12. Contrary to Baker (1987), 167, who declines to consider nonreductive physicalism on the ground that "such a view, at least until developed further, seems to lack bite" (9, n. 11).
13. See further Kincaid (1988).
14. Nagel (1979), 166.
15. Locke (1964), III, iv, 11; first edition, 1690.
16. Due largely to J. Allan Hobson and Robert McCarley; see Hobson (1988).

17. Hobson (1988), 15, 18.
18. Jackson (1982).
19. Churchland (1985), 22–28, who also argues that the blind-from-birth omniscient neuroscientist *could* imagine what it is like to see scarlet.
20. Churchland (1985), 10–14, 25.
21. Nagel (1979), 172.
22. Nagel (1979), 166.
23. Nagel (1979), 169.
24. Nagel (1979), 171.
25. Nagel (1979), 175.
26. Nagel (1979), 175.
27. Post (1987), 247–248.
28. Contrary to Nagel (1979), 165; cf. 210.
29. Mackie (1977), 15.
30. Joseph Schumpeter, quoted with approval by Rorty (1989), 46.
31. Kant (1969), Ak 389.
32. So named by Mackie (1977), 38–42, who presents a slightly different version from the one here.
33. Sartre (1956), 625.
34. Mackie (1977), 41.
35. Nozick (1981), 17.
36. Millikan (1984), Chs. 1–2; see also Millikan (1989).
37. Kavka (1985), 317; see also Kavka (1986).
38. Axelrod and Hamilton (1981); Axelrod (1984); Campbell (1985); Axelrod and Dion (1988).
39. Axelrod (1984), 87.
40. The following argument is developed in more detail in Post (1987), Ch. 6.
41. Berlin (1969), 172.

7

GOD

IDEAS OF GOD

Does God exist? Ostracism or worse is often the punishment for those who dare to ask. Yet metaphysicians are compelled to ask. A theory of what there is would hardly be complete if it said nothing about whether God is. A theory of being *qua* being would hardly be complete if it said nothing about whether to be is to be in some relation to the divine—whether, for example, to be is to be created and sustained by God. Moreover, metaphysicians are compelled not only to ask whether God exists but also to treat the answer as anything but a foregone conclusion. Their calling requires them to accept nothing merely on faith or on authority or out of inertia or conformity to received opinion. They are to follow the evidence and argument wherever they lead, however unpopular the conclusion. There have been times and places where the punishment for this questioning attitude is death. In our own time there are still such places.

Another hazard for those who would bring evidence and argument to bear on whether God exists is that there are so many ideas of God. According to one idea, the divine nature is personal, as for example in Christianity, Judaism, Islam, and an important strand of Hinduism. According to another idea of God, the divine nature is nonpersonal, as in a different strand of Hinduism, and in Theravada Buddhism. Some think of God as a Being who rules the world and acts in history. Others deny this, as do Neoplatonists, Stoics, Deists, Buddhists, and

Hindus of the Advaita-Vedānta school. According to some religions, deity becomes incarnate in the world. According to others it does not. And is the Bible the Word of God, or rather the Qur'an, the Bhagavad Gita, the Book of Mormon, or none of these?

We seem to encounter a hopelessly irreducible plurality of conflicting ideas of God. If asked whether you believe in God, the only reasonable reply may be, "Which one? There are so many." Theists according to one religion may be atheists according to another. It is unsettling to reflect that had we been born in another part of the world, our religion would probably have been very different from whatever it happens to be. Had I been born in India, I would probably have been a Hindu; in Sri Lanka, probably a Buddhist. Not so for our science: Engineers the world over use the same mathematics and physics.

Such reflections suggest to some that there is no truth of the matter in religion, so that impartial evidence and argument do not apply. One way they reach this skeptical conclusion is by a kind of argument from disagreement. The long history of interminable disputes over conflicting religious claims is best explained by there being no culture-independent reality for them to be about. Instead, people's ideas about God grow out of their diverse temperaments, languages, and histories. Furthermore, or so we may be told, *this* argument from disagreement *can* be backed by a queerness argument, and indeed by a broadened AQ. For the alleged truth of a religious claim is not derivable from, reducible to, or even nonreductively determined by what all would agree *is* objectively there. Hence the relation of supposed religious truths to culture-independent reality is quite mysterious. Better by far to regard religious claims as expressing subjective responses to the problems we all face so often in this difficult and sometimes terrifying world.

Theists might respond roughly as moral realists respond to arguments from disagreement. The amount of past religious disagreement is greatly exaggerated, they may say. Furthermore, in today's world of rapid communication and interaction, diverse religious traditions consciously learn from each other and seem gradually to be converging. Above all, there may be an equally good if not better explanation of the religious differences:

Consider the hypothesis that the great religions are all, at their experiential roots, in contact with the same ultimate divine reality, but that their differing experiences of that reality, interacting over the centuries with the differing thought forms of differing cultures, have led to increasing differentiation and contrasting elaboration.[1]

The history of differences and disputes would thus be explained by reference to different perceptions or awarenesses of the same transcendent reality.

As for queerness arguments, theists may say, it remains to be shown, despite some prejudice to the contrary, that religious truth is not determined by what is objectively there. If there is an ultimate divine reality, it too is objectively there, in the sense of having an existence independent of our culture-bound ideas about it. Surely such a reality would determine the truth of religious claims. Morever, we must not neglect the possibility that the truth of at least some religious claims can be derived from ordinary objective features of the world. Some of the classical arguments for the existence of God attempt to do so, as we'll soon see, and they have their defenders. Nor should we neglect the possibility that even if religious truths cannot be derived from objective features of existence, nevertheless religious truth is nonreductively determined by them.[2]

Skeptics might concede the possibility that eventually some such strategy will be found that works. But until then, we have no good reason to believe either that some religious claims actually can be derived from or determined true by ordinary objective features of the world or that there actually exists an ultimate divine reality that determines religious truth. Indeed, skeptics claim that we have good reason to doubt there is any such reality. For each religion views what it regards as the Holy as demanding an absolute response of faith, worship, and deed, to the exclusion of all that is incompatible with such response. "Within Christianity, for example, this absoluteness and exclusiveness of response has been strongly developed in the doctrine that Christ was uniquely divine, the only Son of God, of one substance with the Father, the only mediator between God and man."[3] This means that believers must regard their own distinctive claims as true and those of incompatible faiths as false. The different religions cannot all be true, and any evidence for the distinctive truth of one is automatically evidence for the falsity of all the others. Since the evidence includes the religious experience and testimony of the believers within each religion, it follows that for any given religion there is always more such experiential and testimonial evidence for its falsity than for its truth.

Generalizing, skeptics go on to point out that *any* evidence or argument against other religions will automatically be evidence or argument against your own, unless you can point to some relevant difference in virtue of which what counts against those others does not count against yours. The burden of proof therefore falls heavily on believers for giving some reason to suppose that there actually exists an ultimate divine reality answering to their distinctive idea of such a reality. It will not do to spell out the alleged relevant difference between your religious beliefs and those others by appealing to the authority of Scripture, to revelation, to faith, to your own experience or that of cobelievers, and so on. For these are exactly the same kinds of things alien believers will point to in defense of *their* beliefs.

In view of all this, we may be forced to conclude that the greatest challenge to theism does not come from atheism, "secular humanism," or reductive scientific philosophies, as is often supposed. The greatest danger may lie in the apparently irreducible plurality of conflicting theisms and the skeptical or agnostic questioning the conflict gives rise to. The reason so many believers do not realize this, says the skeptic, is that they are ignorant of, because they chauvinistically insulate themselves from, the great religions and cultures of the world other than their own.

IS THE IDEA OF GOD COHERENT?

Skepticism also feeds on arguments to the effect that our idea of God is just logically incoherent. For example, there is an old puzzle connected with the idea that God is all-powerful, or omnipotent; there is nothing God cannot do. But surely there *are* things God cannot do, since God cannot make something both round and square at the same time or make a rock larger than God can lift. One solution to this puzzle, due essentially to St. Thomas Aquinas (1224–1274), is to explain that what God's omnipotence means is simply that God can do whatever does not involve a contradiction in terms and that inability to pull off a logically contradictory feat spells no limit at all on anyone's power, God's included. As Aquinas puts it, "Nothing which implies contradiction falls under the omnipotence of God."[4] God's power meets no obstacle here, "because nonsense remains nonsense even when we talk it about God."[5]

But there is another puzzle, brand-new, that seems far more serious. This concerns God's omniscience, according to which God knows every truth whatever. That is, for any proposition p, if it is true that p then God knows that p. Recently a powerful argument has appeared that purports to show the logical incoherence of the idea of omniscience.[6]

Let us call the infinitely many true propositions God knows the t's. Like any propositions, the t's can have various properties P. For example, a given proposition t can have the property of being about this or that, being simple or complex, being a divinely revealed truth, or whatever. Now imagine that the t's and at least some of the properties P are arbitrarily paired with each other in a *1-1 correlation*: To each t there corresponds just one P, and to each of at least some of the P's there corresponds just one t. To illustrate a 1-1 correlation, think of a theater in which all the seats are taken and there are no standees. When that happens, seats and patrons are in a 1-1 correlation or pairing with each other.

In such a correlation or pairing of t's and P's, it can happen that the property P with which a given t is paired is a property of t itself, or it can happen that this P is *not* a property of t. To illustrate the latter possibility, consider the simple proposition that $2 + 2 = 4$. This is surely among the t's (the propositions God knows), and it might be paired with a property it does not have, such as the property of being complex. If so, this proposition, that $2 + 2 = 4$, would not have the property with which it is paired, being simple rather than complex.

It turns out that there must necessarily be *more* properties P the t's can have than there are t's. That is, for any given correlation or pairing of P's and t's, there will always be a property P the t's can have which is paired with no *t* whatever and which must therefore be a leftover. For an example of such a property, consider the property D* defined as follows:

D* is the property of being a *t* that does not have the property with which *t* is paired.

If we suppose that this property D* is *not* a leftover, we are supposing that D* is paired with some *t* or other. But to suppose that D* is paired with some *t* leads to a contradiction.

To see that it does lead to a contradiction, call the *t* with which D* is supposed to be paired t*. Either t* has this property D* with which it is paired or not. Suppose t* does have D*. Then by the definition of D*, t* has the property of being a *t* that does not have the property with which it is paired. Since the property with which t* is paired is D*, it follows that t* does not have D* after all. So t* does not have D*. But if t* does not have D*, it does not have the property with which it is paired. This entails, by the definition of D*, that t* has D* after all. So t* both has and does not have D*, and the supposition that D* is paired with some *t* leads to this contradiction. Hence D* must be a leftover.

This means that there are more properties P the propositions *t* can have than there are *t*'s. That is, *there are more such properties P than there are propositions God knows*. By itself, this result does not count against the notion of omniscience. The trouble comes when we conjoin this result with the fact that *there are as many truths as there are properties P.* The reason there are as many is that for each such P there is a true proposition. For example, there is the proposition that P is a property or that P is a property the *t*'s can have or that P is or is not a property of some given proposition *t**. Since there are as many truths as there are P's, and there are more P's than propositions God knows, it follows that there are more truths than God knows. The idea of an omniscient being is logically incoherent.

This argument is said to be "Cantorian," because it borrows a strategy invented a century ago by the mathematician who founded set theory, Georg Cantor. The strategy enters into the definition of

D*. Cantor used a similar definition to prove what we call Cantor's Theorem. Cantor's Theorem says that given any set S, then even if S is infinitely large, the set of subsets of things in S is larger still. One can see the parallel between Cantor's Theorem and the statement that given the set S^t of propositions God knows, even though S^t is infinitely large, the set of properties of propositions in S^t is larger still.

There is also a Cantorian argument that there can be no totality of all the truths.[7] Given any such alleged totality and given any supposed 1-1 correlation between the propositions in it and the properties they can have, we can use D* to define a property left out of the correlation. We then conclude that because for each such property there is a true proposition, not all the true propositions can be in the totality. The notion of such a totality is incoherent. If we define God's omniscience not as in the second paragraph of this section, but as meaning that God's knowledge constitutes the totality of the truths, our definition inherits this incoherence.

Another way a Cantorian argument might have an impact on one's idea of God is via the notion of *self-existence*. God is often said to be self-existent, meaning that the explanation of why God exists lies not in the existence and power of something else but in God's own nature. It is of God's *essence* to exist; God exists by a necessity of God's own nature. This in turn is often construed to mean that in every possible world whatever, God exists. But what is a possible world? A number of contemporary philosophers identify a possible world with the totality of propositions true in that world.[8] Indeed, this way of construing possible worlds is useful in other contexts as well. But if there can be no totality of truths, there can be no totality of truths that counts as a possible world. Insofar as our idea of God's self-existence rests on some such notion, it will be incoherent.

Theists seem to have a relatively easy reply here: So much the worse for this notion of a possible world. Let possible worlds be construed in some other fashion, perhaps simply as ways this world might have been. Of course we must go on to explain what sort of thing (if any) a way the world might have been is, but logical incoherence seems not to lurk in this direction.

Unfortunately, there may be no easy reply to the problem about omniscience. How can the theist define God's omniscience or all-knowingness without landing in incoherence? There are ways to do so, but they all seem to pay a high price. One way is to reject the Cantorian strategy involved in definitions like that of D*. But this would require us to give up a form of reasoning that seems perfectly sound in this and other contexts, a form of reasoning that in addition underlies important parts of logic and mathematics we need for other purposes.

Another way out is to require the truth-bearers to be *sentences*, not propositions; what is true or false is not a proposition but a sentence. The advantage of sentences is that each is built step by step from a listed vocabulary by a finite number of applications of listed rules. This means there can be at most a *countable* infinity of sentences, which is to say that they can be counted by placing them into 1-1 correlation with the integers 1, 2, 3, ... As before, a Cantorian argument shows there are more properties P the truth-bearers can have than there are truth-bearers; there is an *un*countable infinity of such properties. But because the truth-bearers are now *sentences* and because there can only be a *countable* infinity of them, it follows that it is *not* the case that for each such property P there is a truth, meaning a true *sentence*, even though for each such P there is a true *proposition*. This blocks a key step in the preceding argument—the step, There are as many truths as there are properties P. This step is sound when the truths are propositions, unsound when they are sentences.

Thus we could coherently define God's omniscience to mean that for any sentence ϕ, if ϕ is true then God knows that ϕ is true. But there is a high price to pay. Limiting the truth-bearers to sentences restricts what God can know to what can be expressed by a sentence. Many would insist that God's knowledge should not be limited to what can be so expressed. Surely there are inexpressible truths, and surely they are known fully by God.

For this reason and a number of others, some theists are likely to propose a completely different way out. These fussy exercises in logic are irrelevant, they may say. We should *expect* to find that much about God transcends our logical understanding, because God's nature is infinite or unlimited. God's nature and existence are therefore matters not of reason but of faith. What reply could metaphysicians make to this?

FAITH AND REASON

From the belief that something is infinite or unlimited, it might or might not follow that much about this something transcends our logical understanding. It does not follow that logical reasoning has no application at all. For example, suppose you believe in an infinite being, but you also believe that a certain claim your opponents make about this being is self-contradictory, hence logically incoherent. Showing where and how their claim is incoherent would involve a process of logical reasoning.

A self-contradictory claim cannot be true, not even of God. Since believers want their claims about God to be true, they will therefore refrain from knowingly making such claims. They will recognize with C. S. Lewis, himself a believer, that "nonsense remains nonsense even when we talk it about God." If they think the claim in question is *not* self-contradictory, they will normally look for a flaw in any argument that purports to show it is self-contradictory. To look for a flaw in some such troublesome argument requires one to engage in a process of reasoning. This is clear from attempts to find a way out of the Cantorian argument against omniscience. Such exercises in logical reasoning can hardly be irrelevant.

On the other hand, nothing said so far entails there is no room for faith. One way faith might enter is by the believer's trusting that even if no flaw has yet been established in the troublesome argument, eventually one will. Or the believer might trust that even if nobody ever finds a flaw, there is one somewhere. Such trust derives from the conviction that God exists and has unlimited powers, including omniscience. This conviction, this faith, is to override any logical difficulties, momentary or perennial, in understanding precisely what God's infinite nature entails.

All this is true even when the troublesome argument is not that a certain claim is self-contradictory but that it conflicts with contingent fact. For example, the Biblical account of how God created the world and its living things, if taken literally, conflicts with Darwin's evolutionary account. If the latter is fact, the former cannot be literally true. Recognizing that this is so requires one to draw inferences from both the Biblical language and Darwin's. It requires one to engage in a process of reasoning, however elementary.

The same is true of attempts by theists to find a way out of the difficulty posed by evolutionary accounts. The way out, according to many theists, is to concede that whatever the evidence for an evolutionary account may have been a hundred years ago, today the evidence is overwhelming. Such an account is not mere theory or speculation, but fact. Therefore, the Biblical account cannot be literally true. Nonetheless, it contains the essential truth that God is the Creator, even if the way this truth is expressed is colored by the rudimentary science or nonscience of those who strove to record that which was revealed to them. We must learn to distinguish their rudimentary and inessential mythology from the core of divinely revealed truth they imperfectly expressed. That is, we must learn to "demythologize" as we interpret Scripture.

Fundamentalists will have none of this. The Biblical account *is* literally true. It is Darwin and his ilk who must go. Thus fundamentalists work hard to find flaws in the evidence and argument for an evolutionary account. The world was created just a few thousand years ago, they believe, not the billions required for life to appear and evolve into its present forms. Each species was created much as it is now. Fundamentalists are compelled by such beliefs to explain away the evidence from radioactive dating of geological strata, from the astrophysics of planet formation, from the fossil record, from molecular genetics, and more.

What animates fundamentalists and nonfundamentalists alike in their attempts to find a way out of the challenge from evolutionary accounts is of course faith, in particular the conviction that God is the Creator. They trust that somewhere or other there is a flaw in any argument that proceeds from what evolutionists tell us are the facts to the conclusion that God the Creator does not exist. This trust, this acceptance, is to override any and all counterargument. *Nothing* will ever be allowed to count against belief in God the Creator.

Defenders of the need for faith—also called *fideists*—sometimes advance *reasons for the limits of reason*, or a rational excuse for irrationality.[9] They argue that *everyone* is logically compelled to take something on faith, even the most extreme rationalist. The rationalist believes that a belief is acceptable only if it has been rationally justified. Fideists object to this rationalism in two related ways. First, the rationalist's own belief, if it is to be acceptable in accord with the very standard it sets, must itself be rationally justified. But it cannot be rationally justified, the fideist contends, since there is nothing from which its truth could be inferred—there is no further and more fundamental principle that could be cited in justification. The rationalist's belief is therefore itself a matter of faith. Sometimes this objection to rationalism is called the *tu quoque* (You're-one-too) argument.

The second objection amounts to a kind of regress argument for fideism. In order to justify a belief rationally, we must cite some evidence from which we can infer its truth or at least the likelihood of its truth. But this evidence must itself be rationally justified, which requires us to cite some further matter from which it can be inferred, and so on. In order to put an end to this regress, we must eventually accept something without being able to infer it from anything more fundamental. That is, we must accept something without rational justification, which is to say on faith.

Both the *tu quoque* and the regress argument for fideism presuppose that rational justification is *foundational*. According to foundationalists, rational justification is a matter of inferring the truth or at least the probable truth of a belief from some further matter or matters that are themselves justified. This regress must end, and it ends in something that cannot itself be inferred from anything more fundamental. But whereas fideists hold that this something must be accepted irrationally, on faith, foundationalists hold that it may be accepted rationally. For even though it is not *inferentially* or *mediately* justified—not justified by being inferred from anything further—it is *non*inferentially or *im*mediately justified. Whatever is thus *immediately* justified is said to be at the foundation or basis. A belief is rationally justified if it is either at the basis or can be inferred from what is at the basis.

Foundational rationalists therefore reject the regress argument for fideism. Indeed, they turn it into a regress argument for foundationalism. The only way to put an end to the regress of justifications, they think, is to recognize that there are immediately justified beliefs and that our knowledge can be based on them. As for the *tu quoque*, foundational rationalists must of course argue that the rationalist position itself is either at the basis, hence immediately justified, or else inferrable from what is at the basis.

Fideists often respond with an argument straight out of the skeptic's armory. The skeptic begins by asking what criteria are to be used in classifying a belief as immediately justified or basic. Not just any old belief will do. If it is to be an adequate basis or foundation, the belief must be, if not certain, at least substantially more secure than what is based on it. It must at least be rather more likely to be true than false. Foundationalists therefore need some criterion both for selecting beliefs that in this way deserve to be at the foundation and for excluding those that do not.

But when we look at all the different criteria foundationalists have so far proposed, says the skeptic, we notice something disturbing. We notice that beliefs that satisfy the criteria have often turned out to be false, so far as we can tell given today's evidence. This includes beliefs that satisfy such criteria as clarity and distinctness, intuitive obviousness, sensory obviousness, impossibility of conceiving otherwise, inherent plausibility, and so on and on. History is littered with the corpses of cherished basic beliefs passionately defended on the ground that they satisfy some such criterion.

The skeptic concludes that unless we can specify some relevant difference between our present basic beliefs and those others, we have no reason to suppose that just because they satisfy the criterion they will not go the way of those others. Finding rotten apples in a barrel does not mean all are rotten. But unless we know that the proportion of bad apples to good is relatively small, we have no warrant for supposing that the next apple from the barrel is more likely to be good than bad. And how could we know this? That is, how could we know, in the case of a criterion for inclusion at the basis, that the proportion of untruths to truths certified by the criterion is relatively small? Evidently we could know this only by means of *another* criterion, one that tells us which of the beliefs certified by the first criterion we are warranted in calling true. But this just raises the same problem all over again.

This "problem of the criterion," as it is called, leads skeptics to conclude that nothing whatever is known, because nothing has sufficient rational justification to count as knowledge. Therefore, we should suspend belief. Fideists, on the other hand, are led by the problem of the criterion to conclude not that we should suspend belief but that we must accept certain theological matters on faith, as true. We *do* have knowledge of such things, via faith. *Relativists* deny that we have any knowledge. Because there is no rational way to adjudicate beliefs at the basis, so-called "knowledge" is merely relative to whatever a person or culture happens to start with by way of basic commitments. "None of the above!" say the foundational rationalists. Skepticism, fideism, and relativism are all mistaken. There *are* secure foundations, even if they are sometimes hard to make out.

This four-way quarrel among skeptics, fideists, relativists, and foundational rationalists has droned on for centuries.[10] And it has seemed interminable. A good policy, then, would be to look for a presupposition all four parties share that gives rise to the quarrel, a presupposition without which the quarrel would lose much of its point. One presupposition the parties seem to share is that rationality is foundational. The debate is largely about how best to stop the regress of justifications and how to respond to the problem of the criterion. This problem is at its most acute at the foundations. Reject the idea of foundations, then, and the problem should ease dramatically if not disappear. Indeed, the four-way debate would lose much of its point. Or so *non*foundational rationalists will urge.

What does nonfoundational rationality look like? There are several varieties, most of them elaborated in the last thirty years. What they have in common is a rejection of the notion of *im*mediately justified beliefs. There is no such basis. The way to stop the regress of justifications is to recognize that the so-called "immediately" or "noninferentially justified" beliefs—those that seem in this way to be foundational—are themselves mediately or inferentially justified. But what justifies them is *not* some yet more basic set of beliefs, appeal to which would just lead to further regress. Rather, they are justified by their "coherence" with the totality of our beliefs. Their justification rests in part on the "less basic," general beliefs whose justification led us to look for foundations in the first place. In some sense, the less basic beliefs are supported by the more basic, and the more basic by the less. Our beliefs do not form a pyramid resting on some foundation unjustified by reference to anything else. Instead, they form a web or net of mutually supporting nodes, with some nodes having more threads running from them than others, and some in contact with the world.

Coherentists, as these nonfoundational rationalists are called, often argue that the history of science bears out their view of justification. In the sciences, a general hypothesis or theory is first invented to account for various observations, which form part of the support for the theory. If the theory is a good one, it is confirmed to a high degree by these observations and by further observations made in order to test both it and its competitors. As our confidence in the theory grows, we often turn around and judge observation by reference to the theory itself. Observations that would falsify the theory are explained away.

For example, confidence in Copernicus' sun-centered theory of the solar system grew to be rather high among many astronomers within about half a century of its publication in 1543. But the theory entailed that the observed positions of the stars should be different when the earth is at opposite sides of its orbit about the sun. Sirius, for instance, should appear to be in one place in June and a slightly different place in December, much as the direction of the press box changes for those moving around a race track. Attempts to detect this "stellar parallax" had all failed. Such failure, unexplained, would falsify the theory, as anti-Copernicans emphasized. But instead of rejecting the theory, Copernicus and his successors explained the failure to detect stellar parallax by arguing that the stars are vastly more distant than anyone had imagined and that existing instruments were therefore unable to detect it. They turned out to be right, and stellar parallax was finally detected nearly three hundred years later, in 1838. Had they turned out to be wrong, as often happens when a new theory is proposed, the theory would have had to be rejected or revised to accommodate the recalcitrant observations.

This process of mutual adjustment between observation and hypothesis, between data and theory, goes on all the time in the sciences, as we attempt to find "the best overall data-theory fit" or some kind of provisional equilibrium between our theories and our considered observations. The equilibrium is *provisional* because new data, new phenomena, even new arguments from the old can cause us to change our minds about a belief, however justified our confidence in it may have been in light of earlier evidence. Nothing is permanently immune to revision. Nothing may be sheltered from testing or criticism simply by appealing to authority or to faith.

One can develop a version of coherentism that emphasizes this revisability or fallibility of all beliefs, in and out of the sciences, its own included. A belief is rationally acceptable only if it has so far survived rigorous testing and criticism in the ongoing process of forging a coherent equilibrium between beliefs and evidence. Furthermore, this "critical coherentism," as we may call it, takes the fallibilism so far as to grant that even the most highly justified beliefs need not be true and need not even be more likely to be true than false. This is to grant the skeptic that we have no criterion for truth or even for probable truth.

But contrary to the skeptic, we are not therefore to suspend belief. Instead, we are to accept those beliefs that have so far survived in the ongoing critical process lately sketched. We are not to accept them as true, let alone as certainly true and in that sense as knowledge. We are not even to accept them as more likely to be true than false. We are to accept them as having so far survived in the ongoing critical trial and in that sense as superior to those of their predecessors and competitors that have not. The survivors may not be any more likely to be true than false, but they *are* more likely to be true than their failed competitors, so far as we can tell from the evidence to date.[11]

When in their turn the survivors fail, we revise or replace them with something better. According to the critical coherentist, the alternative to certainty, or even to probable truth, is not the skeptic's suspension of belief; not the relativist's "anything goes" or "so many people, so many opinions"; and not the fideist's leap of faith. Nor is it the foundationalist's insistence that there are immediately justified beliefs on which we may base claims to truth or at least to probable truth. The correct alternative is the ongoing critical trial or process of adjudication that allows us to sort beliefs into better and worse—into those that have so far survived and those that are false so far as we can now tell.

Critical coherentism will distance itself in this way from skepticism, relativism, fideism, and the foundational picture of rationality they tend to presuppose. The regress problem is solved, critical coherentists will argue, by means of the so-called basic beliefs themselves' being inferentially justified in a coherent, criticizable equilibrium of theory and evidence.

What about the *tu quoque*, the argument that the rationalist's own position cannot be rationally justified and must therefore be held on faith? Critical coherentists will argue that whatever the fate of foundational rationalism in this regard, a critical coherence version of rationalism does satisfy its own standard. For it is itself revisable and fallible, has so far survived criticism, and coheres with the rest of our justified beliefs in reflective equilibrium.[12]

Too good to be true? Perhaps. But unless fideists can show that not even this account of rationality can be rational by its own standard, they will not be entitled to claim that *everyone*, even the rationalist, is logically compelled to take some matters on faith. At best they will be entitled to claim that *foundational* rationalists are so compelled. Thus fideists will no longer be entitled to appeal to the *tu quoque* as providing a rational excuse for irrationality.

On the other hand, none of this shows, nor is it meant to show, that fideists can and ought to be persuaded simply by rational argument and evidence to become rationalists. Unless I already concede the relevance of rational argument and evidence and am open to being persuaded by it, I cannot and need not be so persuaded. Unless I am willing to accept the results of argument, I cannot be argued into anything, or out of it.

This seeming refusal ever to let argument and evidence bear on the faith can be deeply disturbing, even to many theists. Such faith is blind, in the sense of not being guided, or revisable, by reasoning either from conditions independent of the believer's state of faith or even from the counsel of fellow human beings who are not so sure. Fideism appears to claim that at least as regards fundamental religious beliefs, blind faith is supreme as the way to certitude and salvation.

What is disturbing about this attitude is that it may seem scarcely distinguishable from fanaticism. The fanatic is one who goes ahead regardless of any contrary counsel or caution, one who will not be swayed. The fanatic thus breaks off a crucial kind of communication or discourse with others, one that accords them equal respect in the weighing of opinion and action. Fanaticism tears at the fabric of community and solidarity. So too does fideism, if and insofar as it vilifies the counsel of others deemed beyond the pale. Conceivably, if improbably, Luther (1483–1546) had no such extremes in mind when he called reason "God's worst enemy . . . the devil's bride . . . a beautiful whore," and said, "Reason must be deluded, blinded, and destroyed" and "faith must trample under foot all reason, sense, and understanding."[13] But Luther's antirationalism is a recurring theme in Protestantism, and there are extremists who take him at his word.

Moderate fideists, by contrast, allow that reason can and must play a role in the search for religious truth. In their view, it is neither unexpected nor scandalous that the expression of faith should occasionally adjust itself to the achievements of reason, science included. They can agree with Kafka: "All human error is impatience, a premature renunciation of method, a delusive pinning down of a delusion." Of course, like all fideists, moderate fideists trust that the methodical pursuit of argument and evidence will not result in the refutation of the core beliefs of their faith, or even in their fundamental revision. In order to see whether they are right, one must look to the arguments.

ARGUMENTS FOR THE EXISTENCE OF GOD

We have already encountered one of the classical arguments for the existence of God (in Chapter 4). This is the "cosmological (or first-cause) argument": Since the universe exists contingently and since every contingently existing thing has a cause or explanation in the existence and power of something beyond, it follows that there must be some creator, which is God. In one version or another, the cosmological argument appears in the writings of Greek, Arabic, Jewish, and Christian philosophers and theologians, including Plato, Aristotle, al Farabi, al Ghazali, ibn Rushd, Maimonides, Aquinas, Spinoza, and Leibniz. Whatever persuasiveness the argument may have derives in large measure from a kind of commonsense or reflex belief that because the universe might not have existed, there must be some reason why it does.

In Chapter 4 we noted that the argument presupposes a version of the principle of sufficient reason. We also noted that whatever the evidence for PSR may once have been, today PSR cannot be assumed without considerable argument, and probably not even then. The evidence from quantum physics for *un*caused events at the micro level counts heavily against PSR. So too does the application of quantum theory to the universe as a whole, at its earliest state, when it is even smaller than an electron. Such application, via "tunneling," implies that the universe had an uncaused or spontaneous beginning.

Even if these and other considerations against PSR are not conclusive, they do show that PSR can no longer be used, undefended, as an assumption in arguments for the existence of God or in any other arguments. Even if PSR could be assumed, still the cosmological argument need not persuade. For even if we were entitled to conclude that the existence of the universe does have an explanation or cause, we would need to establish that this cause is one and the same as the God of Scripture.

Another classical argument for the existence of God is the "design argument." The argument begins by noting the wonderful complexity of plants and animals and their adaptation to their surroundings and each other. Giraffes have long necks for feeding on the leaves of acacia trees, horses have enlarged nostrils for breathing hard while on the run, and so on, in countless other cases. In each case, the creature is exquisitely designed for the conditions in which it finds itself. The only adequate explanation of this marvelous design and adaptation, this intricate order on such an enormous scale, is the creative activity of God. God gave giraffes long necks so they could reach the leaves. Arguments like this enjoyed considerable popularity in the eighteenth century, when it seemed that scientific discoveries were testifying to, rather than detracting from, the fullness and wonder of God's creative activity (contrary to what Berkeley had feared). But design arguments soon received a powerful critique in Hume's *Dialogues Concerning Natural Religion* (1779). One of Hume's several objections was that theists had not shown there is no equally good, nontheistic explanation of the adaptation and apparent design of living things. Hume was right, but it was only later, with the appearance and subsequent elaboration of Darwin's theory of evolution, that many people began to realize there might well be an equally good explanation, and indeed an explanation in purely natural terms. The adaptation, the apparent design, the wonderful, teeming variety and complex order of living things can all be explained by natural selection operating over vast stretches of time on differences generated by random mutations in the living things' genetic material (the material we now know as DNA). Unless theists can show that this explanation is not as good as one that posits a designer, the design argument fails.

Design arguments have another problem, also targeted by Hume. Suppose that some such argument were to succeed in showing there is a divine designer. Then the divine mind that does the designing, being itself a case of wonderful design and order, would itself be as much in need of explanation as the natural order. What designs the designer? Theists often reply that God is a *necessary* being, one whose existence and properties are explained by the being's very essence or nature, a self-explanatory being. This reply raises two further problems. One is the problem of what warrants identifying the alleged designer with a necessary being, God in particular. Why couldn't the designer be some very powerful but nonnecessary being, indeed a nondivine being, even an evil one? This problem parallels one we saw for the cosmological argument: What, if anything, warrants the assumption that the first cause is identical with the God of Scripture?

The second problem has to do with the very notion of a necessary being. Do we really understand what it means to say that the explanation of the existence of something lies in that something itself? There are philosophers who claim that this idea is incoherent, that it makes no sense to talk of a self-explanatory being. Bertrand Russell was such a philosopher: "The explanation of one thing is another thing." Explanation is an intelligible concept when we apply it to concrete cases of the sort that give rise to the concept, where the explanation or cause of why something occurred or came into existence is always in the causal power of something else. We stretch the concept out of shape when we try to apply it to cases where this is not so. It makes no sense to say that the explanation of the existence of a thing lies in its own nature. Theists who invoke such a notion, in order to cut off questions about why God exists, are merely playing a word game in order to salvage a shaky argument.

Theists may reply that this misconstrues the relevant notion of a necessary being. The core idea, they may say, is that of a logically necessary being, one whose existence is logically contained in the nature or essence of that being. To ask why such a being exists is like asking why a bachelor is unmarried. Just as being unmarried is logically contained in the very concept "bachelor," so is existing contained in the very concept of God. The explanation of why God exists, like the explanation of why bachelors are unmarried, lies in a necessary connection—in the one case, between the essence of bachelorhood and being unmarried; in the other, between God's essence and existence. To persist in asking why God exists is to reveal that you do not understand the concept of God, just as to persist in asking why bachelors are unmarried shows that you fail to grasp the concept of bachelorhood.

One response to this is to recall Quine's arguments against the very distinction between necessity and contingency. If Quine is right, the very notion of necessity presupposed in talk of a necessary being would have to be rejected. Recall also anti-essentialist theories of being *qua* being, discussed briefly in Chapter 1. According to anti-essentialism, there is no necessary connection between a being *qua* being and any property it may have. Hence there can be no necessary connection between God *qua* God and the property of existing, even if we assume that existence is a property.

Some theists are in a position to make short work of this anti-essentialist objection. They may say that talk of a necessary being does not commit them to essentialism. Their claim is not, or need not be, that God *qua* God exists. Rather, the claim is that just as necessarily anything that has the property of bachelorhood is unmarried, so too is it necessary that anything that has the property of Godhood—anything that has the properties or nature God has—exists. But a successful reply to Quine is another matter, requiring not only a detailed rebuttal to his arguments but also a positive theory of meaning and truth that supports the relevant notion or notions of necessity and contingency. Some theists think they have such a theory, one that enables them to explain where Quine goes wrong. Others are less sure.

What might lead theists to say that God is a necessary being, other than that doing so gets them out of some trouble with the design and the cosmological arguments? The main motivation, going back at least to St. Anselm (1033–1109), grows out of the Biblical conception of God as a supreme being. God is a being "than which nothing greater can be conceived," as Anselm put it, a being so perfect that it is impossible for there to be one yet more perfect. Thus by definition God is maximally perfect, in a sense that entails moral perfection, omnipotence, and omniscience, among other perfections. Anselm then argues that a being that did not exist would be less perfect than one that does, so that existence, being a perfection (and therefore a property), is necessarily contained in God's nature as a maximally perfect being.

Indeed, this is the heart of Anselm's "ontological argument" for the existence of God. That God exists follows from our very concept of God as a maximally perfect being. A being that existed only in our minds, only as a concept, would be less great than one that has actual or real existence. Since by definition God is a being than which none greater can be conceived, God must have actual or real existence. This ontological argument, in one form or another, has intrigued philosophers off and on ever since it appeared in Anselm's work. The most recent resurgence of interest has occurred in just the last thirty years, with the application of new methods from what is called "modal logic," which attempts to formalize various notions of possibility and necessity.

One objection to the ontological argument, due to Kant, is that existence is not a property, hence not a perfection. It is true that 'exists' behaves grammatically like a predicate in such sentences as 'God exists', or 'Elvis exists'. In this respect, 'exists' is like 'swims', 'flies', and other predicates, as in 'Jones swims' and 'Smith flies'. Nevertheless, despite this surface resemblance in the grammar, the function of 'exists' is very different. When we use a predicate such as 'swims' or 'flies', we do so in order to *describe* something; we do so in order to attribute a property to it—the property of swimming or flying. But when we use 'exists' we add nothing to our concept of the thing; we add no property. Instead, we merely posit the thing as being an object that has the properties that *are* involved in our concept. " 'Exists' offers no description but merely as it were puts the item mentioned into the picture."[14]

It follows that a being that exists does not have, for that reason alone, some further property or perfection beyond the properties and perfections it would have were it not to exist. However rich our concept of a being, we cannot infer from the concept alone that the being exists. According to Kant, "Whatever, and however much, our concept of an object may contain, we must go outside it, if we are to ascribe existence to an object."[15]

There is another objection to ontological arguments. They begin by assuming that we can at least conceive of a maximally perfect being; such a being is at least possible. This assumption is explicit in a sophisticated ontological argument constructed in our time by Alvin Plantinga. "*Maximal greatness*," he says, "is possibly exemplified."[16] A being has maximal greatness just in case it not only has "maximal excellence" but also has maximal excellence in every possible world. A being has maximal excellence just in case it has moral perfection, omnipotence, and omniscience—that is, just in case it is maximally perfect.

But is it really true that such a being is at least possible? After all, the notion of omniscience, as we saw earlier, may well be logically incoherent. If it is, it cannot possibly be exemplified, and the same then holds for maximal excellence, which entails omniscience, and for maximal greatness, which entails maximal excellence. The basic premise of ontological arguments would be false. It is true that there are ways out of Grim's Cantorian argument against the coherence of omniscience, but as we also saw they come at a high price—too high, in the view of many.

Suppose the idea of an omniscient being is logically incoherent and with it the idea of a maximally perfect being. Then the theist's motivation for calling God a necessary being would be in trouble. The motivation, as lately seen, starts with the Biblical conception of God as a supreme being. This is interpreted to mean a being than whom none greater can be conceived, which according to Anselm entails existence. Hence God exists necessarily; God is a necessary being. But if a supreme being must be omniscient, as seemingly it must, the starting point of this rationale would inherit the incoherence of omniscience. Some other way of motivating the idea of a necessary being would have to be found if theists want to meet the accusation that they invent the idea simply in order to get out of some trouble with the design and cosmological arguments.

Are there any other arguments for the existence of God? A number have been given, but they are generally thought to be less substantial than the cosmological, design, and ontological arguments. For example, there are moral arguments for the existence of God, according to which the existence and nature of morality can be adequately explained only by reference to God's existence and nature. The trouble is that there seem to be equally good if not better explanations, some of them in purely natural terms, as we began to see in the last chapter in connection with the question of whether there are any objective values.

Arguments from religious experience seem to fare no better. Let the experience be your own or shared by many others, and let it be as overwhelming as you like. Even so, any inference is problematic which moves from the existence and character of such experience to a supernatural or transcendent reality either responsible for or answering to it. One problem with the inference is the sheer variety of religious experiences within the different religions and the often conflicting accounts of their nature given by those who have them. The difficulty here resembles those we saw earlier in connection with the apparently irreducible plurality of conflicting ideas of God. The variety seems to many to point not to a single underlying reality but to a plurality of incommensurable subjective states.

Another problem is this. Suppose that the religious experiences, or a special class of them, proved after all to share some invariant feature. We would still need to show that the only explanation of this, or at least the best explanation, is in terms of some transcendent reality. But there are alternative explanations, and some of them seem at least as good if not better. One such explanation is that if we indoctrinate enough people, from childhood, to believe in a transcendent reality and to see everything in those terms, as is done in most of the world's religions, we can expect that a number of people will actively seek what they have been taught is the highest possible form of experience and that some will undergo such experience whether they actively seek it or not. Others, lacking indoctrination or resistant to it, will not have the experience. If you put in a certain way of seeing and experiencing, you get it out. What is responsible for the experience is ultimately the indoctrinated person's internal state, not some transcendent reality experiencible even by a neutral or "uncontaminated" observer. Unless some such explanation can be excluded, an explanation in terms of a transcendental reality cannot be assumed without argument to be the best.

On balance, the traditional arguments for the existence of God, taken individually, seem to most philosophers and theologians to be not at all compelling. But what if they are taken not individually but collectively? Even if no one of them is compelling, perhaps each contributes some degree of support, so that when added together they push belief in God over the top. Unfortunately for this line, an argument based on a false premise or an unsound inference provides zero support for its conclusion. If, as their critics claim, these arguments for the existence of God are all based on a false premise or an unsound inference, each contributes zero support. Adding zeros yields only zero.

Theists might reply by saying that even though there are no compelling arguments *for* the existence of God, there are also no compelling arguments *against*. Hence we are free to believe in God. This reply faces two problems. One is that there might after all be compelling arguments against the existence of God, as we see in the next section. The other is that the failure or nonexistence of any arguments *for* a belief can itself amount to a strong argument *against* it.

For example, suppose I believe there is a large, shaggy, shy, humanoid creature living in remote areas of the Pacific Northwest. Suppose further that even after many years of searching, by many people, none of the alleged evidence for the existence of Bigfoot survives scrutiny. The photographs, footprints, hair, bones, and sightings are all examined at length, and all prove to have explanations in other terms—as hoaxes, commercial promotion, honest mistakes, other animals. After a time—decades, perhaps—the failure of any such evidence or argument for Bigfoot begins to add up to a strong reason for believing there is no such thing. Such a creature should leave traces. If we find no traces, probably there is no such animal.

God too is supposed to leave traces. If none of the alleged traces survives scrutiny—if after centuries of searching, none of the arguments from the alleged traces to the existence of God stands up—why should we not conclude that probably there is no such being? "Faith," replies the fideist. According to the moderate fideist, at least, so long as there are no compelling arguments against the existence of God, belief in God is self-certifying in a way that belief in Bigfoot or any other mere creature is not. But what exactly is it about belief in God that is supposed to win it exemption from the testing to which we subject belief in Bigfoot or any other being? Why couldn't members of other and conflicting faiths also exempt *their* beliefs from questioning in this way? What is so special about your faith, other than that it is yours? And *are* there no compelling arguments against the existence of God?

ARGUMENTS AGAINST THE EXISTENCE OF GOD

The most disturbing argument against the existence of God, even from the point of view of the believer, is the "argument from evil." Bad things happen to good people, indeed horrible things, occasionally on an inconceivable scale. Some of these evils are inflicted by fellow human beings, as at Auschwitz. Others have nonhuman or natural causes, as when a massive earthquake, followed by flood and then fire, shattered Lisbon one morning in 1755, when the churches were crowded to honor the dead on All Saints Day. Horrors like these have caused many believers to question and even to abandon their faith. If God is all-powerful and loving, how could He allow so many innocent people to suffer so terribly?

This anguished question forms the existential root of the argument from evil. The argument comes in two versions. One aims to show that the traditional theist's beliefs form a logically inconsistent set and that to avoid the inconsistency one must give up belief in God. This is to raise the *logical* problem of evil. The other version of the argument is more modest, claiming only that the evidence makes God's existence unlikely. This is to raise the *evidential* problem of evil.

Those who raise the logical problem of evil often begin by agreeing with the traditional theist that evil exists and is real. Some religions deny this, holding that what we call evil—even intense pain—is only an illusion. But Judeo-Christian theism is firmly committed to the reality of evil. This is true even when evil is defined as the absence or privation of good. The privation itself is no illusion but actually exists or occurs; the privation of good at Auschwitz was as real as anything gets. Indeed, many theists take pride in honestly and unflinchingly facing the reality of evil.

It is then pointed out that evil can exist only if God is either unwilling or unable to prevent it. But by definition God is omnipotent, hence able to prevent it. So God must be unwilling. But this is inconsistent with God's being perfectly loving. Those who love their children do not willingly allow them to suffer. The only way out of this inconsistency is to abandon belief in a God who is omnipotent and perfectly loving.

Traditional theists are committed both to God's being omnipotent and to the existence of evil. So they must reply to this argument by denying that God's perfect love or goodness entails that God must always want to prevent evil. Just as those who love their children must sometimes let them suffer in order that they may learn and grow, so too does God rightly allow suffering in order that we may all learn and grow. The world is a place of soul making, and soul making requires that we successively confront and overcome various evils in order to grow in strength and wisdom.

The trouble with this appeal to a "soul-making theodicy," as it is called, is that it is compatible with the existence of only so much evil as is necessary for soul making. There seems to be far more evil in the world than is necessary for this end. Is it really necessary that millions of children should die over the centuries—from earthquake, flood, fire, disease, famine—simply in order that others may grow in wisdom? Could this end possibly justify such harrowing means? What would we say of parents who allow some of their children to sicken and die, even though they can afford the necessary preventive care, simply in order that their other children may watch and learn and grow?

Theists often reply with the "free-will defense": The evils in question result from our misuse of the free will God gave us. God lovingly created us as autonomous, free beings, knowing full well that we might abuse our freedom by choosing evil ways. It is we who choose to go to war, to build concentration camps, to settle where the risk of natural disaster is known to be high. Were God to prevent such evils by causing us to choose otherwise, we would not be genuinely free. The idea that we could both be caused to choose a certain way and also choose freely is self-contradictory. Since "nothing which implies a contradiction falls under the omnipotence of God," as Aquinas says, the idea that God cannot prevent the evils we freely choose is consistent with God's omnipotence.

One problem with the free-will defense is that many evils seem not to result from the misuse of free-will. For example, there are unforeseen and unforeseeable natural disasters for which no human agent is responsible. Theists sometimes reply that such disasters are visited on us because of the sins of an ancestor, so that a human agent is responsible after all. But this implies that God, who is supposed to be loving and just, sometimes inflicts intense suffering and death on otherwise innocent people—children included—for something that happened centuries earlier. Again we are forced to ask what end, what higher good, could possibly justify such harrowing means.

Theists may reply that even if it seems to us that there could be no such higher good, it is at least logically possible for there to be one. And theists do seem to be on strong ground in arguing that it is at least logically possible for there to be a higher good even God can achieve only by creating a world in which there are free human creatures and a large amount of evil. If this *is* logically possible, the existence of such evil is consistent with God's omnipotence and perfect love. Unless someone can show that this is *not* a logical possibility, the logical problem of evil cannot be said to yield a successful deductive proof of the nonexistence of God.

The *evidential* problem of evil is another matter. Those who press the evidential problem concede the logical possibility of there being some higher good even God can achieve only by creating a world in which there are free creatures and a large amount of evil. Instead, they argue that on balance the evidence supports the opposite view: God could have created a world containing substantially less evil without eliminating any higher good. One important piece of evidence to this effect is animal suffering. Think of a fawn trapped in a forest fire, badly burned, lingering in agony for days before death ends its suffering.[17] The fire was started by lightning in a place so remote that no human could have witnessed the blaze, let alone put it out. Surely an omnipotent and omniscient being could have prevented or at least reduced the fawn's suffering without jeopardizing some higher good, including human free will.

Of course one cannot prove beyond doubt that this is true, but it seems unlikely that there is some higher good an omnipotent, omniscient being could bring about only by allowing the fawn to suffer. Even if we could think of some higher good that is made possible only by the fawn's suffering, there would remain many *other* instances of intense, apparently pointless suffering, animal and human. Is it reasonable to believe that *none* of them could have been prevented even by an all-powerful, all-knowing being without eliminating a higher good?

When we consider [this] more general [question] in light of our experience and knowledge of the variety and profusion of human and animal suffering occurring daily in our world, it seems that the answer must be *no*. . . . The idea . . . seems an extraordinary, absurd idea, quite beyond our belief.[18]

Theists might reply that there are strong rational grounds for believing in God, grounds that are independent of these considerations about the significance of evil. If these grounds are strong enough, we have more reason to believe there is an omnipotent, omniscient, perfectly loving God than to believe there are evils such a being could have prevented without eliminating some higher good.[19]

The difficulty with this reply is that the various attempts to provide independent, rational grounds for believing in God—the traditional arguments for the existence of God—seem to many to be not at all compelling, individually or collectively. As we saw in the last section, the traditional arguments are all in trouble—the ontological, design, and first-cause arguments, and the arguments from morality and from religious experience. Unless something better can be produced, many think we do have more reason to believe there are evils God could have prevented without eliminating some higher good than to believe there is an omnipotent, omniscient, perfectly loving God. And this leaves out of account both Grim's Cantorian argument against the coherence of the very idea of omniscience and the fact that the failure or nonexistence of any arguments *for* a belief can itself amount to a strong argument *against* it.

There is another argument against the existence of God that deserves our attention. Theists often bring in God in order to explain various happenings. In the first-cause argument, God is invoked in order to explain why there is a world. In the design argument, God's creative activity is said to explain the origin of species and their marvelous adaptation to their surroundings. Morality, religious experience, and miracles are also said to be explained by the existence and activity of God. In short, God is thought to play an essential explanatory role in our account of the existence and properties of our world and of much that occurs in it. Such a God is a God of the explanatory gaps.

This opens up what might be called the "argument from explanatory excess" against the existence of God. In each case where reference to God is said to be needed to explain some state of affairs, runs the argument, a better explanation is now available, indeed an explanation in purely natural terms. The origin of the world, of life in all its variety, of morality, of religious experience, and more have now all been adequately explained in natural terms or are at least on the way to being so explained. We need not posit some additional, supernatural entity in order to account for the phenomena. Such an entity would be explanatorily superfluous, a gratuitous extra, an excess. Since we ought not multiply entities beyond what is necessary to explain things, it follows that probably there is no God.

The argument from explanatory excess combines inference to the best explanation with a principle of economy. Inference to the best explanation is used frequently not only in science and ordinary affairs but also, as we have seen, in theology. If certain phenomena are best explained by some account, divine or otherwise, we infer that this account is probably true. Suppose that the footprints in the garden, the broken window, the rifled safe, and the empty beer can on the kitchen table are best explained by positing an unhurried burglar. We may then infer that probably there was such a burglar. Positing a *second* burglar would go beyond what is necessary to account for the phenomena; doing so would be to multiply entities beyond necessity. Therefore, probably there was no second burglar. A principle of economy is involved here, according to which we are not to multiply entities beyond necessity. This principle is called Ockham's razor, after the fourteenth-century Scholastic philosopher who used it in order to dispense with a number of entities he deemed superfluous.

Theists have two main lines of reply to the argument from explanatory excess, neither of them easy to sustain. One is to argue that the phenomena in question have *not* been adequately accounted for in natural or other nontheistic terms and are not even on the way to being thus accounted for. We must posit God in order to explain what needs explaining. Since positing God in this way does not multiply entities beyond what is necessary to get the explanatory job done, Ockham's razor is blunted.

What makes this line hard to sustain is that it requires showing that the sciences have not closed and are not even on the way to closing the relevant explanatory gaps. Much of the evidence suggests the contrary (as we noted in this and in earlier chapters). Also, such a line assumes that God is a God-of-the-gaps, and thereby renders belief in God vulnerable to scientific and other advances that close the gaps. It places theism in direct competition with science over the kinds of explanatory power pursued by the sciences. If it is objected that the sciences cannot explain why anything at all exists, an obvious rejoinder is that the question of why anything at all exists is based on a false presupposition, a position we encountered in Chapter 4.

The other line of reply to the argument from explanatory excess is to argue that belief in God is not a matter to which Ockham's razor applies, indeed not at all a matter of the kind of explanatory power pursued by science. God is not a God-of-the-gaps, and theism is compatible even with the closing of every scientific explanatory gap. What makes this line hard to sustain is that so much of the theist's own talk about God seems to be inconsistent with scientific explanation, as we noted at the end of Chapter 4. Talk of divine miracles and creation, for example, seems to entail that the explanation of such matters is in terms not of natural processes but of the supernatural activity of God. Talk of God seems inherently to be talk of an extra entity, one in excess of the natural entities posited by the sciences, hence an entity to which Ockham's razor should apply.

The thinking theist is therefore confronted with a dilemma. Either God is a God-of-the-gaps or not. If God is a God-of-the-gaps, then Ockham's razor is very keen, in view of the enormous and growing explanatory power of the sciences and, the sciences aside, of other nontheistic accounts of the world. On the other hand, if God is not a God-of-the-gaps, hence not a matter to which Ockham's razor could apply, then it is hard to make sense of the theist's own talk about God in connection with miracles, creation, and much else.[20] Whether there is some way out of this dilemma lies at the heart of one of the great issues of our time: how to reconcile belief in God with the growing explanatory power of the sciences and with the naturalistic view of things this growing power may imply.

NOTES

1. Hick (1983), 115.
2. In the manner sketched by Post (1987), Ch. 8.
3. Hick (1983), 117.
4. *Summa Theologica*, Ia Q xxv, art. 4.

5. C. S. Lewis (1962), 28. I am indebted to Tim McGrew for recalling this passage.
6. Grim (1988); Grim (forthcoming), sec. 4.5.
7. Grim (1984).
8. For example, Adams (1974); Plantinga (1976); and Plantinga (1974). A Cantorian argument against this notion of a possible world appears in Loux (1979), 53.
9. Bartley (1984) explains this fideist strategy and reasons for rejecting it.
10. Popkin (1951); (1959); (1979).
11. Post (1987), secs. 1.3–1.6.
12. Post (1971), (1983), considers some of the difficulties in the way of arguing this and how a moderate Quinean version of critical coherentism might overcome them.
13. Quoted in translation by Kaufmann (1963), 75.
14. Mackie (1982), 46.
15. Kant (1933), Transcendental Dialectic, Bk. II, Ch. III, sec. 4.
16. Plantinga (1974), 214.
17. Rowe (1978), 88.
18. Rowe (1978), 89.
19. Rowe (1978), 90–94.
20. Post (1987), Ch. 8, proposes a way around this difficulty.

METAPHYSICS AND MEANINGFUL EXISTENCE

We know too well what can destroy meaning. Holocaust, the slaughter of war, social and economic collapse, starvation, torture—all these and too many more can render one's life meaningless. Meaninglessness itself can add to the casualties by sapping the will to live. A few may endure the worst, their faith and hope intact; many more cannot. You and I, comfortable in some belief in the meanings of our lives, may think those who lost faith could not have had a very strong one; their failure was somehow a moral failure as well. To this there is the survivor's unanswerable reply: You were not there, you cannot know what it was like, you too would have succumbed. All your beliefs, all your vaunted theories, metaphysical or otherwise, could not have saved you.

Metaphysical theories, like religious beliefs, are sometimes powerless to buoy us through cruel extremes, meanings intact. Moreover, some varieties of metaphysics can themselves destroy meaning. They work on us more gently, if insidiously, not by physical force but by ideas, often in slow degrees over long periods of time. We remain free, in our capacity as rational, autonomous individuals, to weigh and accept or reject the ideas as we see fit. True, certain philosophies are sometimes wielded by the unscrupulous to justify questionable use of force. But philosophy's guiding spirit is to accord equal respect to one's fellow human beings in the weighing of opinion and action. It's just that some philosophers think that when opinion is properly weighed, we must conclude that existence is meaningless.

Their idea is that, objectively speaking, the world contains no meaning because it contains no value. What we call "value" and "meaning" are but projections of our subjective moods and passions onto what in fact is value-neutral, inert, or dead. Because "the will itself, taking the inner view, craves objective reasons" for the meaningfulness of existence[1] and because there are no objective reasons, existence is meaningless. There are no objective reasons because there are no objective values, and there are no objective values because values cannot be reduced to or derived from what *does* have objective existence. If the world is the totality of fact and if there are no normative facts, there is no value in the world but only in us. As regards value and meaning, "This world is but canvas to our imagination," if we may use Thoreau's words to this effect.

A related line of thought accompanied the rise of modern science, as we saw in Chapter 6. The new physics in particular led many to think that what really or primarily exist are extension, mass, force, impact. Any properties or qualities of a thing that cannot be reduced to these have only a derivative or secondary existence. This emphatically includes values, which often came to be thought of as even more subjective than such secondary qualities as a thing's color, sound, and taste. Values, purpose, and meaning seemed to form no part of the real world. The real world appeared to be value-neutral, inert, no longer enchanted.

This attitude remains very much alive. Thus we hear from a distinguished contemporary physicist that "the more the universe seems comprehensible, the more it seems pointless."[2] A distinguished philosopher asks, "Science has helped us to know and understand this world, but what purpose or meaning can it find in it?"[3] He answers that the scientific world picture robs us of meaning in the sense of a purpose given us by some nonhuman source. And another contemporary philosopher suggests that in a naturalistic metaphysics, human endeavor viewed objectively must seem to shrivel and to be vilified. He asks, "Can the vocabulary of life as 'meaningful' or 'meaningless' still play a role in a naturalistic interpretation of things?"[4]

What underlies this skepticism about value and therefore about meaningfulness and enchantment is of course the argument from queerness, or AQ, as we learned to call it in Chapter 6. Because any alleged objective values are neither derivable from nor reducible to the descriptive or natural properties, their relation to what does have objective existence is decidedly mysterious. Objective values must be very queer sorts of things. Better by far to replace them with some sort of subjective response that can be causally related to stimulation by the objective features on which the alleged objective values are said to depend. What we call objective values are but our subjective responses spread by imagination on the clean canvas of the world. Such enchantment as the world enjoys we must summon from within and project outward.

But we saw how AQ overlooks the possibility of a relation of *nonreductive* determination between the descriptive features and objective values. Even when AQ is broadened to take account of non-reductive determination, it remains unconvincing. It neglects a number of theories that connect value to various objective features in such a way as to imply nonreductive determination of the former by the latter. Furthermore, the defeat of AQ makes room for a positive argument for the determinacy of valuation. The objective features of things in the world, ourselves and our histories included, can non-reductively determine the values. There can be an objective truth of the matter as regards value, even when the truth is so complex or emotional that we cannot ascertain what it is.

So too for the meaningfulness of existence, insofar as this is a matter of how existence is to be valued. The world contains value and meaning after all, not because value and meaning prove reducible to or derivable from objective features but because they are nonreductively determined by them. This world may be but canvas to our imagination, in the sense that no value or meaning of things is reducible to or derivable from any description, so that none can thereby be read off from the description. Yet thanks to the nonreductive determinacy of valuation, there are objectively better and worse ways of spreading our emotions on the canvas, in the sense that some are determined as correct and others are not.

Which ones are correct is another matter, often dauntingly complex, requiring subtle forms of argument and evidence scarcely touched on in this book. For example, how would one argue for or against the correctness of a vision of the universe not as inert or dead—and not as a place of reptilian indifference to us and our fate—but as an enchanted place of belonging, wonderous and alive?[5] How would one argue for or against the correctness of various other religious visions of existence?

But even though questions like these would require at least another book, note that we have reached the point in this one at which they may be taken seriously. The presupposition on which they are based—that there is objective correctness here, however difficult to ascertain—is both compatible with the pursuit of metaphysics and supported by arguments any metaphysician might use. Theorists of being *qua* being need not hold that to be is to be value-neutral, inert, or dead and need not speak of what there is only in the indicative. Instead, they may speak in the rich tapestry of other moods needed to express the values and meanings of what there is.

A *physicalist* theory of being *qua* being, of all things, affords an illustration. Nonreductive physicalists hold that to be is to be composed of entities of the sort physics studies and that all truth is nonreductively determined by physical truth. But this is not to say, as we have seen, that everything is *nothing but* a physical thing. Far from it. The view is compatible with there being many diverse and equally privileged ways things are, including religious ways, some of which often take a kind of priority over the physical. It is compatible also with the objective correctness of value and meaning, including the correctness (assuming it is correct) of a vision of the universe as enchanted and wonderous. We need not be but physical objects sailing in a physical sea.

It is true that physicalism by itself does not entail that there is an objective correctness about these matters, let alone that this vision of meaningful existence in particular is correct. The point, rather, is that when these further claims are conjoined with physicalism proper, the result is a coherent synthesis of physicalism and enchantment which affords an intelligible overall view of a kind of meaning and unity of what there is and our place in it. And if a physicalist metaphysics can lend itself to this sort of synthesis, think how much more easily a number of other varieties of metaphysics can too.

In Chapter 1, we asked whether there could be a coherent metaphysics that not only affords an intelligible view of meaning and unity but also simultaneously rejects all the presuppositions characteristic of traditional metaphysics. Could there be a coherent metaphysics that (i) rejects essentialism and the very idea of *the* way the world is, together with the idea of a privileged vocabulary to express it; (ii) consists of principles that are contingent, *a posteriori,* fallible, and revisable; (iii) involves no commitment to self-evident or other givens and none to the subject as known immediately and fully to itself or as autonomous and disengaged; (iv) avoids not only problematic notions of truth, goodness, and reality but also all talk of foundations; and (v) presupposes no noumenal thing-in-itself beyond the appearances available to common sense and science?

Many philosophers today reject the traditional presuppositions. If they are right to do so and if no coherent metaphysics is possible that rejects them all, metaphysics would be at an end. On the other hand, suppose we were to concede the worst, by conceding (if only for the sake of argument) that the presuppositions should all be rejected. If nevertheless some variety of metaphysics is possible that rejects them all, what would be at an end would be contemporary antimetaphysics. Purified of the objectionable presuppositions, metaphysics could get on with its legitimate perennial tasks.

Again physicalism affords an illustration. There are versions of physicalism, as a review of earlier chapters will confirm, that reject essentialism, privileged vocabularies and unities, claims to necessity, givenness, Platonic and other problematic notions of truth and goodness, foundations, and noumenal things-in-themselves. And once more, if a physicalist metaphysics can thus do without any of the traditional presuppositions, surely there are nonphysicalist varieties that can do so as well. Much contemporary antimetaphysics therefore seems guilty of setting up a scarecrow.

In Chapter 1 we also asked whether there is a constructive variety of metaphysics that meets the challenge of coming to terms with physicalism, either to reject it or somehow to accommodate it. Physicalism meets the challenge, obviously, by way of accommodation, but again there are nonphysicalist varieties that might also meet this challenge. A further challenge was to give a plausible account of the relation between scientific truth and other sorts of truth. A relation of nonreductive determination does the job, according to some physicalists, but not at the expense of other relations in terms of which nonscientific truths can often take priority, as can the varieties of unification they may suggest or support. So too did we see how nonphysicalist metaphysicians could make use of nonreductive determination to much the same effect.

Needless to say, much remains to be done to clarify these and many related matters and to articulate and defend a vision of meaningful existence that is relevant to our perilous situation on this planet. Metaphysical storytellers need have no fear that there is little left for them to do. For the moment, however, it is enough to know that metaphysicians are not just seeing peach blossoms on a mesquite tree in January.

NOTES

1. Wiggins (1976), 341.
2. Weinberg (1977), 154.
3. Baier (1957), 103.
4. Hepburn (1965), 209, 220.
5. Post (1990).

BIBLIOGRAPHY

Adams, Robert Merrihew (1974). "Theories of Actuality." *Nous 17*:211–231. Reprinted in *The Possible and the Actual*, ed. Michael J. Loux. Ithaca: Cornell Univ. Press, 1979, 190–209.

Axelrod, Robert (1984). *The Evolution of Cooperation*. New York: Basic Books.

Axelrod, Robert, and Dion, Douglas (1988). "The Further Evolution of Cooperation." *Science 242*:1385–1390.

Axelrod, Robert, and Hamilton, William D. (1981). "The Evolution of Cooperation." *Science 211*:1390–1396.

Baier, Kurt (1957). "The Meaning of Life." Reprinted in *The Meaning of Life*, ed. E. D. Klemke. New York: Oxford Univ. Press, 1981, 81–117.

Baker, Lynne Rudder (1987). *Saving Belief: A Critique of Physicalism*. Princeton: Princeton Univ. Press.

Bartley, William W. III (1984). *The Retreat to Commitment, 2d ed.* LaSalle, IL: Open Court.

Benardete, José (1989). *Metaphysics: The Logical Approach*. Oxford: Oxford Univ. Press.

Berlin, Isaiah (1969). *Four Essays on Liberty*. Oxford: Oxford Univ. Press.

Buchler, Justus (1978). "On the Concept of 'The World'." *The Review of Metaphysics 31*:555–579.

Campbell, Keith (1988). "Review of Post's *The Faces of Existence*." *Philosophy and Phenomenological Research 49*:358–362.

Campbell, Richmond (1985). "Sociobiology and the Possibility of Ethical Naturalism." In *Morality, Reason and Truth*, ed. David Copp and David Zimmerman. Totowa, NJ: Rowman and Allanheld, 1985, 270–296.

Carroll, William E. (1988). "Big Bang Cosmology, Quantum Tunneling from Nothing, and Creation." *Laval Théologique et Philosophique 44*:59–75.

Churchland, Paul M. (1979). *Scientific Realism and the Plasticity of Mind*. New York: Cambridge Univ. Press.

Churchland, Paul M. (1985). "Reduction, Qualia, and the Direct Inspection of Brain States." *The Journal of Philosophy 77*:8–28.

Collett, T. S., and Land, M. F. (1978). "How Hoverflies Compute Interception Courses." *Journal of Comparative Physiology 125*:191–204.

Copleston, F. C., and Russell, Bertrand (1948). "The Existence of God—A Debate." Reprinted in *Reality in Focus: Contemporary Readings on Metaphysics*, ed. Paul K. Moser. Englewood Cliffs, NJ: Prentice-Hall, 1989, 405–417.

Crane, H., and Piantanida, T. P. (1983). "On Seeing Reddish Green and Yellowish Blue." *Science 221*:1078–1080.

Culler, Jonathan (1976). *Saussure*. London: Fontana.

Culler, Jonathan (1982). *On Deconstruction: Theory and Criticism after Structuralism*. Ithaca: Cornell Univ. Press.

Derrida, Jacques (1976). *Of Grammatology*. Trans. G. C. Spivak. Baltimore: Johns Hopkins Univ. Press.

Derrida, Jacques (1978). *Writing and Difference.* Trans. Alan Bass. Chicago: Univ. of Chicago Press.

Derrida, Jacques (1981). *Positions.* Chicago: Univ. of Chicago Press.

Devitt, Michael, and Sterelny, Kim (1987). *Language and Reality: An Introduction to the Philosophy of Language.* Cambridge: MIT Press.

Ellis, John M. (1989). *Against Deconstruction.* Princeton: Princeton Univ. Press.

Feinberg, Gerald (1966). "Physics and the Thales Problem." *The Journal of Philosophy 63*:5–17.

Goldman, Alvin (1987). "Cognitive Science and Metaphysics." *The Journal of Philosophy 84*:537–544.

Grim, Patrick (1984). "There is No Set of All Truths." *Analysis 44*: 206–208.

Grim, Patrick (1988). "Logic and Limits of Knowledge and Truth." *Nous 22*:341–367.

Grim, Patrick (1991). *The Incomplete Universe: Totality, Knowledge, and Truth.* Cambridge: MIT Press.

Hacking, Ian (1975). *Why does Language Matter to Philosophy?* Cambridge: Cambridge Univ. Press.

Hardin, C. L. (1988). *Color for Philosophers: Unweaving the Rainbow.* Indianapolis: Hackett.

Hawkes, Terence (1977). *Structuralism and Semiotics.* Berkeley: Univ. of California Press.

Heidegger, Martin (1959). *An Introduction to Metaphysics.* New Haven: Yale Univ. Press.

Hellman, Geoffrey, and Thompson, F. W. (1975). "Physicalism: Ontology, Determination, Reduction." *The Journal of Philosophy 72*:551–564.

Hellman, Geoffrey, and Thompson, F. W. (1977). "Physicalist Materialism." *Nous 11*:309–345.

Hepburn, R. W. (1965). "Questions about the Meaning of Life." Reprinted in *The Meaning of Life*, ed. E. D. Klemke. New York: Oxford Univ. Press, 1981, 209–226.

Hick, John (1983). *Philosophy of Religion, 3d ed.* Englewood Cliffs, NJ: Prentice-Hall.

Hobson, J. Allan (1988). *The Dreaming Brain.* New York: Basic Books.

Hooker, C. A. (1981). "Towards a General Theory of Reduction." *Dialogue 20*:38–59, 201–236, 496–529.

Hooker, C. A. (1987). *A Realistic Theory of Science.* Albany: State Univ. of New York Press.

Hume, David (1955). *An Inquiry Concerning Human Understanding.* New York: Bobbs-Merrill.

Jackson, Frank (1982). "Epiphenomenal Qualia." *The Philosophical Quarterly 32*:127–136.

Kant, Immanuel (1933). *Critique of Pure Reason.* Trans. N. Kemp Smith. London: Macmillan.

Kant, Immanuel (1969). *Foundations of the Metaphysics of Morals.* Trans. Lewis White Beck. Indianapolis: Bobbs-Merrill.

Kaufmann, Walter (1958). *Critique of Religion and Philosophy.* New York: Harper Brothers.

Kaufmann, Walter (1963). *The Faith of a Heretic.* Garden City, NY: Anchor.

Kavka, Gregory S. (1985). "The Reconciliation Project." In *Morality,*

Reason and Truth, ed. David Copp and David Zimmerman. Totowa, NJ: Rowman and Allanheld, 1985, 297–319.

Kavka, Gregory S. (1986). *Hobbesian Moral and Political Theory*. Princeton: Princeton Univ. Press.

Kim, Jaegwon (1987). " 'Strong' and 'Global' Supervenience Revisited." *Philosophy and Phenomenological Research 48*:315–327.

Kim, Jaegwon (1989). "The Myth of Nonreductive Materialism." *Proceedings and Addresses of the American Philosophical Association 33*:31–47.

Kincaid, Harold (1988). "Supervenience and Explanation." *Synthese* 77:251–281.

Lentricchia, Frank (1980). *After the New Criticism*. Chicago: Univ. of Chicago Press.

Lewis, C. S. (1962). *The Problem of Pain*. New York: Macmillan.

Locke, John (1964). *An Essay Concerning Human Understanding*. Ed. A. D. Woozley. New York: Meridian.

Loux, Michael J. (1979). "Introduction: Modality and Metaphysics." In *The Possible and the Actual*, ed. Michael J. Loux. Ithaca: Cornell Univ. Press, 1979, 15–64.

Mackie, J. L. (1977). *Ethics: Inventing Right and Wrong*. New York: Penguin.

Mackie, J. L. (1982). *The Miracle of Theism: Arguments For and Against the Existence of God*. Oxford: Clarendon.

Margolis, Joseph (1989). *Texts Without Referents: Reconciling Science with Narrative*. Oxford: Basil Blackwell.

Millikan, Ruth Garrett (1984). *Language, Thought and Other Biological Categories*. Cambridge: MIT Press.

Millikan, Ruth Garrett (1986). "Thoughts Without Laws; Cognitive Science Without Contents." *The Philosophical Review 95*:47–80.

Millikan, Ruth Garrett (1989). "Biosemantics." *The Journal of Philosophy 86*:281–297.

Millikan, Ruth Garrett (1990). "Truth-Rules, Hoverflies and the Kripke-Wittgenstein Paradox." *The Philosophical Review 99*:323–353.

Mortensen, Chris (1986). "Explaining Existence." *Canadian Journal of Philosophy 16*:713–722.

Munitz, Milton (1965). *The Mystery of Existence*. New York: Appleton-Century-Crofts.

Nagel, Thomas (1979). "What is it Like to be a Bat?" In his *Mortal Questions*. Cambridge: Cambridge Univ. Press, 165–180.

Nehemas, Alexander (1987). "Truth and Consequences: How to Understand Jacques Derrida." *The New Republic,* Oct. 5, 31– 36.

Nelson, R. J. (1969). "Behaviorism is False." The *Journal of Philosophy 66*:417–452.

Norris, Christopher (1982). *Deconstruction: Theory and Practice*. London: Methuen.

Nozick, Robert (1981). *Philosophical Explanations*. Cambridge: Harvard Univ. Press.

Passmore, John Arthur (1967). "Logical Positivism." In *The Encyclopedia of Philosophy, vol. 12*. New York: Macmillan, 52–57.

Petrie, Bradford (1987). "Global Supervenience and Reduction." *Philosophy and Phenomenological Research 48*: 119–130.

Plantinga, Alvin (1974). *The Nature of Necessity*. Oxford: Clarendon.

Plantinga, Alvin (1976). "Actualism and Possible Worlds." *Theoria 42* :139–

160. Reprinted in *The Possible and the Actual,* ed. Michael J. Loux. Ithaca: Cornell Univ. Press, 1979, 35–44.

Popkin, Richard H. (1951). "Hume and Kierkegaard." *The Journal of Religion 31:*274–281.

Popkin, Richard H. (1959). "Kierkegaard and Scepticism." *Algemeen Nederlands Tijdschrift voor Wijsbegeerte en Psychologie 51*:123–141.

Popkin, Richard H. (1979). *The History of Scepticism from Erasmus to Spinoza.* Berkeley: Univ. of California Press.

Post, John F. (1971). "Paradox in Critical Rationalism and Related Theories." *Philosophical Forum 3:*27–61.

Post, John F. (1983). "A Gödelian Theorem for Theories of Rationality." In *Evolutionary Epistemology and Theories of Rationality,* ed. W. W. Bartley III, and G. Radnitzky. LaSalle, IL: Open Court, 1987, 253–267.

Post, John F. (1987). *The Faces of Existence: An Essay in Nonreductive Metaphysics.* Ithaca: Cornell Univ. Press.

Post, John F. (1990). "On Reenchanting the World." *Research in Philosophy and Technology 10:*243–279.

Putnam, Hilary (1975). *Mind, Language and Reality: Philosophical Papers, vol. 2.* Cambridge: Cambridge Univ. Press.

Putnam, Hilary (1983). *Realism and Reason: Philosophical Papers, vol. 3.* Cambridge: Cambridge Univ. Press.

Quine, W. V. (1960). *Word and Object.* Cambridge: MIT Press.

Quine, W. V. (1961). "Two Dogmas of Empiricism." In his *From a Logical Point of View, 2d ed.* New York: Harper and Row, 20–46.

Quine, W. V. (1969). "Ontological Relativity." In his *Ontological Relativity and Other Essays.* New York: Columbia Univ. Press, 26–68.

Quine, W. V. (1970). "On the Reasons for the Indeterminacy of Translation." *The Journal of Philosophy* 67:178–183.

Quine, W. V. (1976). "Truth by Convention." In his *Ways of Paradox*. Cambridge: Harvard Univ. Press, 77–106.

Rorty, Richard (1979). *Philosophy and the Mirror of Nature*. Princeton: Princeton Univ. Press.

Rorty, Richard (1984). "Signposts Along the Way that Reason Went." *London Review of Books*, 16–29 February, 5–6.

Rorty, Richard (1989). *Contingency, Irony, and Solidarity*. Cambridge: Cambridge Univ. Press.

Rowe, William L. (1978). *Philosophy of Religion*. Belmont, CA: Wadsworth.

Santayana, George (1957). *Dialogues in Limbo*. Ann Arbor: Univ. of Michigan Press.

Sartre, Jean-Paul (1956). *Being and Nothingness*. Trans. Hazel Barnes. New York: Philosophical Library.

Saussure, Ferdinand de (1966). *Course in General Linguistics*. Ed. Charles Bally and Albert Sechaye. Trans. Wade Baskin. New York: McGraw-Hill.

Smart, J. J. C. (1963). *Philosophy and Scientific Realism*. London: Routledge and Kegan Paul.

Smith, Quentin (1988). "The Uncaused Beginning of the Universe." *Philosophy of Science* 55:39–57.

Taylor, Richard (1983). *Metaphysics, 3d ed*. Englewood Cliffs, NJ: Prentice-Hall.

Vilenkin, Alexander (1982). "Creation of Universes from Nothing." *Physics Letters 117B*:25–28.

Vilenkin, Alexander (1983). "Birth of Inflationary Universes." *Physical Review D* 27:2848–2855.

Walsh, W. H. (1974). "Metaphysics." In *Encyclopaedia Britannica, 15th ed.*, vol. 12. Chicago: Benton, 10–33.

Weinberg, Steven (1977). *The First Three Minutes: A Modern View of the Origin of the Universe*. New York: Basic Books.

Wiggins, David (1976). "Truth, Invention and the Meaning of Life." *Proceedings of the British Academy* 62:331–378.

Wittgenstein, Ludwig (1961). *Tractatus Logico-Philosophicus*. Trans. D. F. Pears and B. F. McGuinness. London: Routledge and Kegan Paul.

INDEX

referential 35
religious 192
semantic 35
subjective/objective 138
Privileged 3, 5, 7, 9, 99
language xvi–xvii, 34
nature of things xv, 192
unifications 102
vocabulary 13, 93
Projectivism 12, 17, 24, 26,
30, 37, 77–83, 190
Proper-function values 148
Protagoras 7, 32
Purpose, biological 50–56, 112,
126, 146, 147
Putnam, Hilary 41, 44, 45
Pythagoras 93

Qualia 131
Quantum indeterminacy 39,
65–67, 85, 88, 90, 105,
174
Quantum theory 39, 65, 67, 85,
88–90
qua problem 48, 53–56
Quine, W. V. 19, 20–23, 28,
40, 42, 44, 45, 47, 48, 52,
53, 55, 176, 177, 188

Rational subject 8
Rationality 9, 64, 66, 73, 140,
149, 167–173
coherentist 170
critical coherentist 171
faith 165–173
foundational 167

logical limits of 167
nonfoundational 169
Realism 30–40, 100
about the world 31–40
about truth 43–59
about value 139–155
absolute version 33, 57, 83
complete description 32
entitivity 83
essentialism 32–35
final theory 38–39
independence 22, 25, 26, 28,
30, 32–39, 43, 58, 77, 79,
80
irony 38
moral 141
nonreductive 36, 58, 77
noumena 37, 80, 81
priority 33–35, 77
quantum theory 39
scientific 36, 38
scientism 36
Reduction 11, 23, 33, 36, 45,
49, 77, 97, 98, 136, 144–
148, 154, 158, 191
Reference 21, 23, 25–30, 35,
42–58, 99
biosemantics 49–59
causal theory 45–49
in/determinate 21–23, 25,
44–58
picture theory 26, 49
resemblance theory 26, 49
Regress problem 167–169,
172
Relational property 32